Josep Llinás

Josep Llinás

Introduction
Alejandro de la Sota

WHITNEY LIBRARY OF DESIGN
An Imprint of Watson-Guptill
Publications, New York

Josep Llinás

© 1997 Tanais Ediciones, S.A., Seville

First published in the United States by Whitney Library of Design, an imprint of Watson-Guptill Publications, a division of BPI Communications, Inc., 1515 Broadway, New York, NY, 10036.

English translation by Hawys Pritchard and Victoria Hughes, edited by Erica Witschey.

Library of Congress Catalog Card Number: 97-60052
ISBN 0-8230-2563-2

All rights reserved. No part of this publication may be reproduced or used in any form or by any means – graphic, electronic, or mechanical, including photocopying, recording, taping, or information storage and retrieval systems – without written permission of the publisher.

Manufactured in Spain

First printing, 1997
D.L.: M-3061 1997

1 2 3 4 / 00 99 98 97

10	There are Times when Friendship Happens First *Alejandro de la Sota*
12	Day and Night *Josep Llinás*
17	**Selected Works**
18	Detached House in Begur
24	Primary Care Hospital in Ripollet
30	Vilaseca Municipal Library
38	Detached House in Sant Feliú de Llobregat
46	Refurbishment of the Barcelona Archaeological Museum
54	Engineering School Library, Lecture Rooms and Departments
64	Office and Apartment Building in Vilafranca del Penedés
68	Apartment Building in Vallcarca
76	Detached House in Can Caralleu
86	Detached House in Colonia Güell
92	Restoration of the Metropol Theater
104	Collblanc Primary School
110	Apartment Building on Calle Carme
118	Computer Department Building
130	Law School Lecture Rooms and Bar
140	Secondary School in Torredembarra
152	Apartment Buildings and Shops in Conegliano
155	**Works and Projects**
170	**Biography**
174	**Bibliography**
176	**Credits**

Josep Llinás begins with some of the last, splendid pages by the late Alejandro de la Sota, which give the keys to the author's personality. Llinás himself is equally successful, in his role as writer and academic, in pointing out some of the concepts with which he maintains an ongoing dialogue in his work as an architect. It was also he who chose the seventeen buildings that make up the core of this book, the *Selected Works*. His attitude towards the choice, however, was always flexible, leaving ample room for suggestions from the publishers and editors, encouraging their creativity with his typical generous understanding. That's the kind of man he is.

Researchers, students and readers will find a detailed inventory of Llinás's output in the documentary section, *Works and Projects*. Under the headings, reference numbers are given to one-off publications (books, catalogues, etc.) or periodicals (journals, etc.) dealing with the building or design in question. The list of publications appears in the very comprehensive *Bibliography,* which comes after the key dates for his career and the abbreviated list of awards and competitions that are summed up in the section called *Biography.*

At the same time as *Josep Llinás* comes out in Spain in the local language, English, German and Italian versions will also be published for the rest of the world. The publishers would like to thank the Subdirectorate General for Architecture in the Ministry of Development, the Spanish authorities in the area, for their constant encouragement to all those furthering the study and practice of architecture and their moral support in the publication of this book. The readers to whom it is addressed will be able to reap the fruits of this collective effort.

The Publishers

There are times when friendship happens first, like an echo of what we are doing. It all started with some reflections on an unposed photograph of a girl in Mies's Farnsworth House, intelligently and sensitively presented by Llinás in an architectural magazine. Then, a Tarragona architect passing in front of the Civilian Government building noticed a stain on the copper of its principal balcony. The architect mentioned it to the Dean of the Tarragona College and the two of them, that very day perhaps, went to see the Governor who explained that Madrid had plans to overhaul the building completely. The stain was just where they had been testing how to clean the copper on the façade which, when we built it years ago, we had so adamantly wanted "dirty." General alert resulted in the architect who built it being called in to restore it – on the condition that he collaborate with a local architect. Luckily, Llinás's name came up. At our first meeting, he was happy to be working with the veteran architect and I, more prophetically, was happy to know that the work would be in excellent hands. He got to know the building better than I did when I built it. If only things could always be like that. He did the same thing with Jujol. Llinás is an intelligent restorer because he is such a fine architect. Then our friendship became so close that we didn't have to bother about professional tuning. And vice versa.

Over the years, I gradually got to know the person and his works, and in him and in them I was thrilled to find an intelligent naturalness, manifest in his exceptional architectonic cogency. All this confirmed his rightness of approach to the Civilian Government building. How could it not?

Our minds work so similarly that it makes one wonder why our buildings aren't more alike. We both already knew that architecture raises a smile, that it is funny, and we put this into practice together many times. Building with things that are "not architecture," turning things and ideas around and making that approach into a worthy way of being an architect, produces buildings – such as the library, the telephone exchange, the museum and many more – which justify an architect fully. That said, though, I see his hidden architectonic suspicions as more obvious and explicit, more philosophical. Fed up with the ordinariness and safeness of these areas, he blithely launches into the dangerous experiment of setting out, fragmenting and playing with a given brief, an impossible site, a recalcitrant property, a change of budget, negligible guidelines, in a complete renunciation of the idea of the finished, exact, architectural object.

Perhaps that is why he accepts impossible commissions such as his involvement in the mish-mash of houses that he's building on unusual plots and locations on the outskirts of Barcelona. There, he apparently sacrifices the whole in favor of pleasant little enclaves of comfort, and in doing so demonstrates his culture and sensibility. When you really get to know them, it is amazing how well resolved and cohesive they are. I wonder if what produces different kinds of buildings in the course of an architect's oeuvre isn't the fact of its being made up of phases rather than of continuous deliberation along ongoing lines. In either case, those of us who follow his progress are kept in a state of constant expectation.

He's the same when he writes. He says things without saying them, sees what no one sees – he saw the Civilian Government building in Tarragona through the sparkling eye of a mentor – and what he says is so densely well said that it stays with you because it makes you think it through over and again.

Dressed in black much of the time, there and yet not there – he lives in Barcelona – he is the intelligent shadow on the stage who says just what needs to be said, no more, no less. He surprises and then stands aside. "Nothing here, nothing there... What is always there is the intelligence, the sensibility, the culture, the humor, and the magician's virtuosity, all the more magicianly the less architect-like it is."

And we have such fun.

Alejandro de la Sota
Madrid, January 9, 1996

Day and Night
Josep Llinás

Some architecture looks work-free, as if the effort of designing, even design itself, has been eliminated from the perception of the finished building, without this implying any simplification of its architectural complexity. As used as I am to doing and redoing projects over and again, often trying out solutions blindly – my focus on any idea that might pull them together having become blurred on paper – I admire this kind of building and this approach to the job. It's an approach within which a throughly honorable aim (relevant, incidentally, to all areas of human activity) is implicit: that of removing work and solemnity from our horizons.

Paradoxically, it seems that the knack of practicing work-free architecture (the journey home) is only achieved through the best part of a lifetime's effort and concentration (the journey out).

Some years ago, I wrote a long article – in *Arquitectura* no. 267 – to the effect that Mies's journey home began during his American period, more specifically in the Chicago apartment buildings at 760 Lake Shore Drive. In those buildings, mind has overtaken hand and Mies's intention, often declared in his writing, of not dealing with problems of form has been realized intact without the mediation of instruments of design. Drawing has been made dispensable, and I conjectured then that he could have explained these buildings to the builder by telephone, without actually appearing on-site, by giving him a (very) few measurements and naming a (very) few materials.

From that point on, Mies rids himself of the instruments of design, and work becomes a game: finding the solution to a project is then rather like solving a crossword or working out a chess move. It's all decided in the mind: the drawing board is at hand, but just as an accessory.

In expectation of that magic moment when the pencil becomes redundant I still remember Alejandro de la Sota's response to my request that he show me a drawing after he had just explained that the stony plinth of the Spanish Embassy building in Paris would be like the bottom of a melting ice-cream: "What do you need it for?" During the building of the Law School lecture-room block, I had a brief encounter with that longed-for moment: it was rather like passing a friend driving in the opposite direction and stopping to say a quick hello.

My intention in that building was to establish a relationship with the natural terrain – soil, grass and trees – much more than with the neighboring buildings or the town. This was the reason behind my decision that the blind walls should be concrete and the roof copper, since they seemed materials that change over time in pace with the rhythms of nature. Conversely, the inactive materials involved in this relationship were not to exhibit any natural attributes: aluminum, industrial fibre-board and high-density block-board.

These materials, which I had never used in quantity before, proved to be something of a revelation (one might almost say a revolution) during construction, turning out to be radically at odds with the result in their resistance to compositive manipulation (the work of the architect).

The appearance of the concrete – concrete is less plastic than it seems, subject as it is to the iron discipline of formwork – is the product of many variables, none of them including my reason for choosing it. Exposure to the elements is what, over time, will determine what it looks like.

The extreme plasticity, and simultaneously the extreme stretchability, of copper sheeting mean that the material forces the installer into introducing a multiplicity of folds and overlaps, so that control over the appearance of the roof – for which I wanted to be responsible – became impossible on any grounds not dictated by the material.

The aluminum panels – governed by strict installation rules and dimensional limitations, so that there is only one optimum solution to angles, for example (folding the panel), and clearances that had to observe a balance between the minimum measurement to allow for expansion and the maximum to avoid letting water in – were the exclusive preserve of the building experts, site surveyors and overseers Jaume Martí and Joan Ardévol.

Etcetera, etcetera, etcetera.

In other words, nature dealt with the concrete; the fitters with the copper; the overseers with the aluminum: the architect as bystander. The result – which I like – is comparable more with the sound of instruments tuning up before a concert than with music.

So. This perhaps over-pedestrian revelation of one of the processes that could have been a homeward-journey discovery for me – using materials that do not change their appearance when built with – was immediately challenged by my experience at the Metropol. There, Jujol, like Mies and Sota as described earlier, also managed to rid the building of the spectre of work, albeit using radically different materials made of water and sand: plastic, semi-liquid, manipulable pastes which, when I saw them in use at the Metropol, reminded me immediately of the dripping stalactites that form when you pick up wet sand and let it run through your fingers.

That transformation of work into play which paves the homeward road seems in this case to have extended to all the skills involved in creating the building.

The proof is to be found in corners and barely visible places inaccessible to the gaze of the spectator and in which, as such, there was absolutely no need for communication.

Take, as an example, the way that plaster has been used on the ceilings, which are formed by the meeting at a 45° apex of angle irons and wooden beams. Hand-applying a mortar mixture to this confluence of lines so as to cover it once and for all, rather than painstakingly plastering around the iron and wood – requiring the trowel to be wielded in difficult places and in an uncomfortable position, arms raised and head tipped back – is both an efficient and splendid solution; this is sensible economy of effort in line with the "work-free" outlook I mentioned at the start.

Plastering reduced to a few minutes the long hours of work that giving a clear account of this junction would have entailed. But while the plaster was still fresh, the plasterer, or Jujol, or someone else – it doesn't really matter – used his fingers to model a pair of eyes, a mouth, a few locks of hair to create a theatrical mask. The message remained a secret because of its lack of visibility, and we only discovered it ourselves halfway through the building work, but in effect someone had subverted the seriousness of work and smuggled play and nocturnal fantasy into the theater.

Later, while the structure was being reinforced in the course of construction, one of the masks came loose and fell to the ground. One of the workmen – there was a strict understanding that anything of Jujol's was untouchable to the point of sanctity – realising how simply the mask was made, decided to make a replacement himself, without telling anyone, hoping that no one would notice the difference.

But he hadn't bargained for a conscientious overseer who spotted it on his first visit to the site, and we made him remove it. Later, though, I wondered if it wouldn't have been better to have left it there after all, even if only to avoid the way we perversely inverted the process of making it (in spare time, as one might do for amusement on an evening), when we removed the failed one and pieced together and fixed the fragments of the original (which the workman had had the foresight to keep) and put it back in place in a painstaking restoration process. Work time instead of spare time.

The whole theater is like that: the palm trees, the bat, the crowns, the letters, the water.

Two different stores: materials which don't need manipulating during building, which install themselves, and materials which are just raw material to be moulded and "animated" during building.

Architecture restrained by construction, or construction upon completed architecture.

Before the parentheses (architecture) or after the parentheses.

Diurnal, intelligent brightness to the point where the mental process enters a building without the mediation of design, or creating without any mediation (design) at all, like sitting by the fire at the end of the day abstractedly making skillful knife-cuts in the wood of a bow and arrow (Tessenow explains the origins of ornamentation with this neat cave-man simile).

Dry, wet. Construction, ornamentation. Intelligence, fantasy.

DIURNAL OR NOCTURNAL. In extraordinary architects – Mies, Sota, Jujol – both of these processes converge in that wonderful end result: work ousted by play.

But one of the processes seems to have lost the battle erroneously waged between these two attitudes – though certainly not by the great architects. The consequences of this defeat are particulary obvious in the way that contemporary architecture is radically incapable of producing ornamentation.

As far as the city of Barcelona is concerned, the nocturnal is exiled in Ciutat Vella. At least I think so after working on the Calle Carme building.

For the entire year that it took to build, the builders used Calle Roig as a lorry-park and unloading area, which meant that at times people had to edge their way between the façades of the houses opposite and the lorry. There were no protests about this, nor about the noise.

At the same time, work began on the Collblanc school, very much in the diurnal territory of wide avenues, traffic lights and office hours.

Difficult neighbors refused to allow the school to use a pedestrian street as the children's access to school, declaring that it was specifically for the dwellings fronting onto it. They won their case.

The nocturnal street as a buffer zone between private domains, or the diurnal street as a marker of property limits.

Especially in Ciutat Vella, this inability to use "nocturnal" devices gives the Calle Carme building, as a piece of architecture, a strange quality of being wedged in by the weight of the language of the avenues. It made me uneasy to be unable to find, in the architecture I have learned, the equipment for producing ornamentation. And I don't mean here ornamentation as historicist alibi. Nor as compulsive or cloying communication. But rather as a friendly, frothy courtesy to others; the sort of courtesy that passengers on a bus might show each other, silent, not talking or communicating, but companionable.

This incapacity made me equally uneasy when the owner of Can Caralleu very sensibly remarked on the lack of the friendly froth element when he saw how the house was turning out. He seemed not to understand an architect's incapacity to introduce that nocturnal dimension into the building.

I tried putting in some colors, but eventually decided against it. We will just have to wait for the trees, plants and insects to establish themselves for companionability to settle into the house.

I genuinely think that schools of architecture should refloat the container of costume jewelry, froth, tomato sauce and fireworks that Le Corbusier consigned to the depths of the sea.

SUMMARY

The architect working at a desk. On the other side of it is architecture.

Mies got rid of the desk, and the pencil and paper along with it.

Jujol did the same by night.

Miesian nights and Jujolian days. I'd encourage students to do things that way... and not to bring back the desk!

Selected Works

Detached House

Carretera Begur a Sa Tuna, Km. 0.8
Begur, Gerona
1978-1980

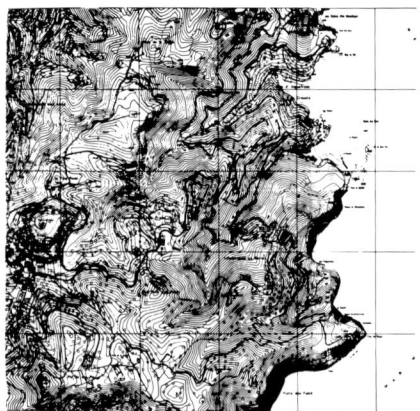

Area map
East façade

The ground on which the house is built was subject to rather obvious constraints: an east-facing slope, a view of the sea from the lower part of the site at the back, and access from the highest point, from the road on the site's western boundary connecting Begur to the beaches.

The site is small (1,000 m² or 10,760 sq ft), as is the house (60 m² each storey), which the design treated as if it were an outbuilding to an imaginary mansion.

It is located on a flattened and paved area, between two relatively low containment walls. Access is via the two headwalls, and the house is connected with the outside through two terraces that are angled to the sun in opposite directions. The passage between the house and the main outer wall at the back is used not only to connect the two terraces outside, but also to provide access to the kitchen and the main door.

The most important decision was to move the internal communication routes from the back to the front façade, so that the access spaces would achieve better views and orientation. The access areas and the living rooms were thus expressed in two different building systems. The living rooms were set within the building's load-bearing and infill walls, while the access areas run through structures based on metal pillars and girders enclosed in glass. In order to protect the large glazed surface area of the gallery, the metal structure was extended outwards and supports a roof of wooden planks.

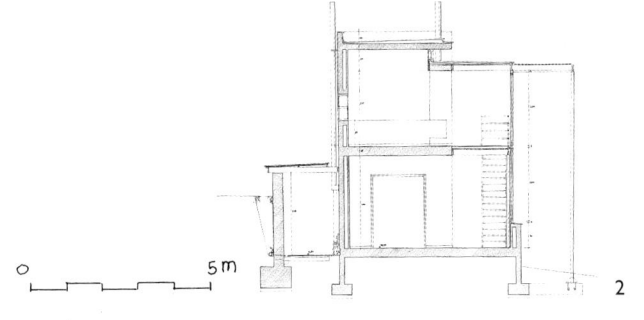

1 South terrace
2 Section
3 Ground floor plan
4 First floor plan

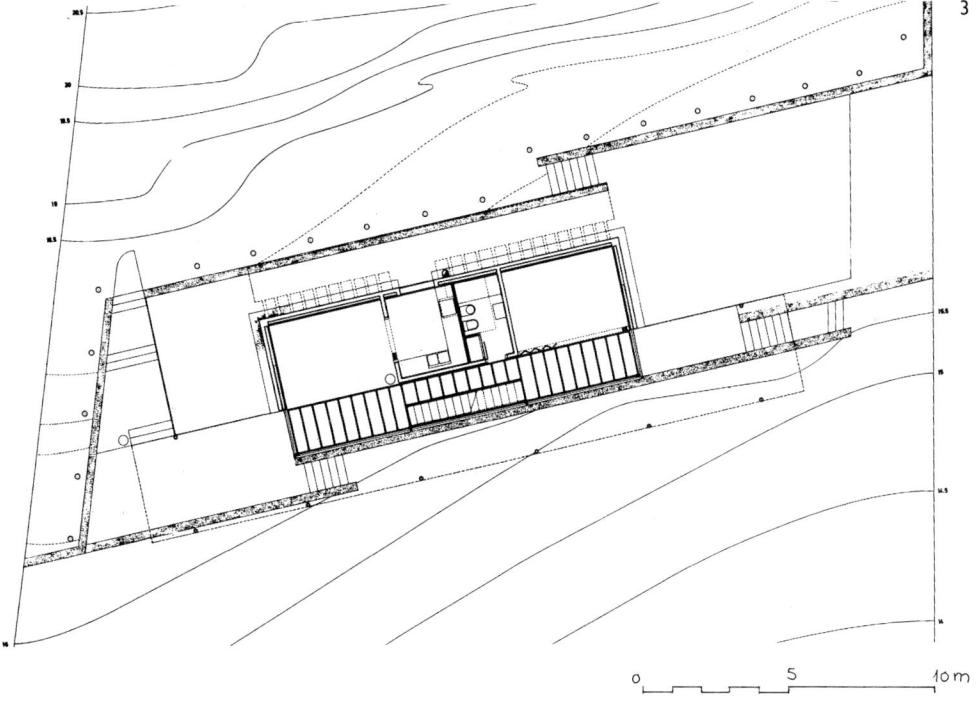

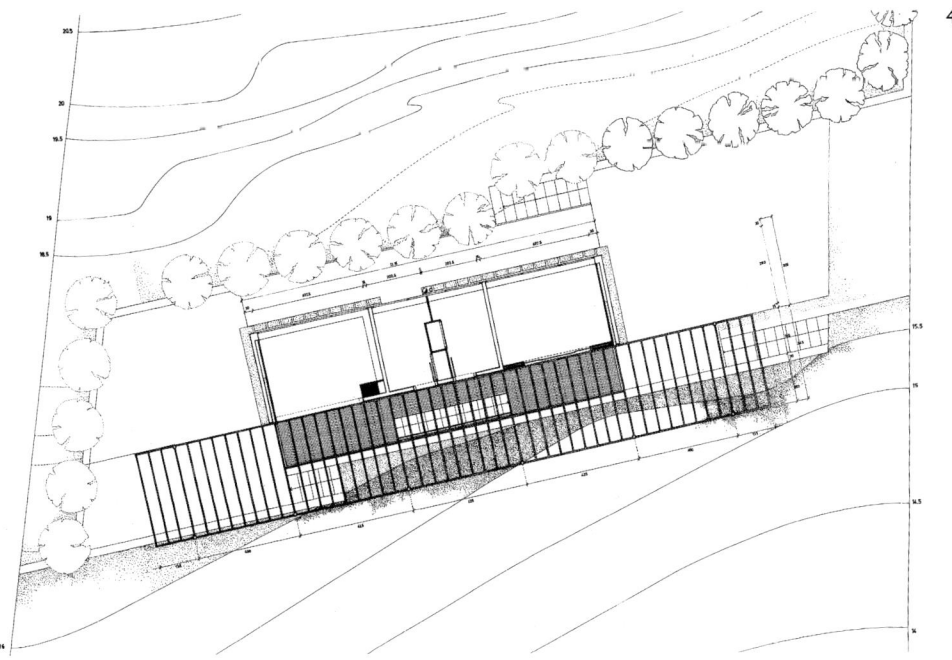

1 Ground floor gallery
2 North façade
3 West façade

3

OWNER José Llinás-Rosa Carmona
SURVEYOR Jaume Martí Almestoy
CONSTRUCTION COMPANY Narcís Fuster, s.a.

Primary Care Hospital

Parque Massot
Ripollet, Barcelona
1982-1985

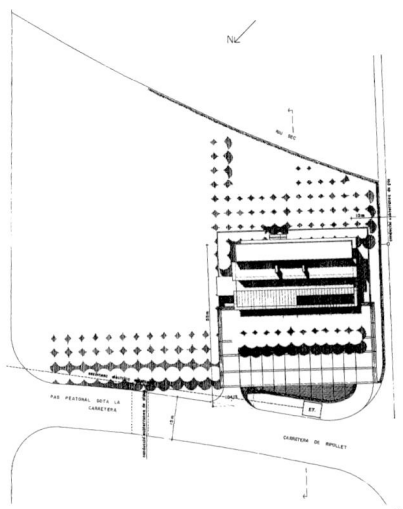

Area map
West façade

The Primary Care Hospital in Ripollet was developed by the Catalonian Regional Government. It is located on a flat site, bounded by the main road between Barcelona and Sabadell, the Barcelona-Terrassa motorway and, perpendicular to this, the local road leading from the main road to Ripollet on one side, and the mostly dried-out riverbed of the River Sec on the other.

The site is some 2.5 m. below the level of the main road between Barcelona and Sabadell and the local road to Ripollet. The area defined by these limits will be developed into a park.

The Special Park Plan stipulated that the hospital building should be placed in a 50 x 50 m. square next to the crossroads of these roads. From the outset, the building was placed in that square, but it was moved as far away from the heavy traffic on the roads as possible, and angled to face the River Sec.

The program also recognized the importance of vehicle access to the site, given its location and boundaries, and set aside a large area for hospital carparks and access to the park.

By building a platform, the problems presented by the large amount of parking space required and the differences of level between the site and roads were both solved at once. Cars could be parked both on it and beneath it, thereby halving the surface area required for the carpark while at the same time placing the access to the building and the roads around the site at the same level.

The building is related to this platform by a staggered section ending in a translucent polycarbonate canopy, while the edge of the platform jutting out next to the building is landscaped, setting the building apart from the road traffic. This gives the construction a much lower profile on approaching it, and its full volume can only be seen from the River Sec side.

1, 2, 5 and 6 Floor plans
3 Cross section
4 North façade
7 West façade

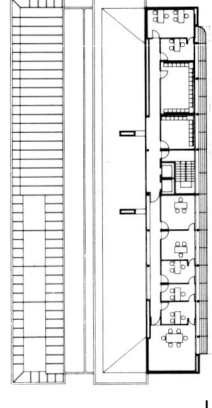
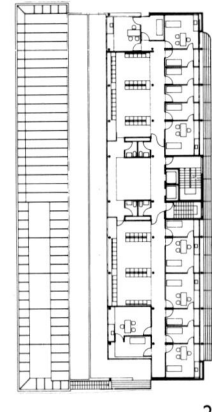
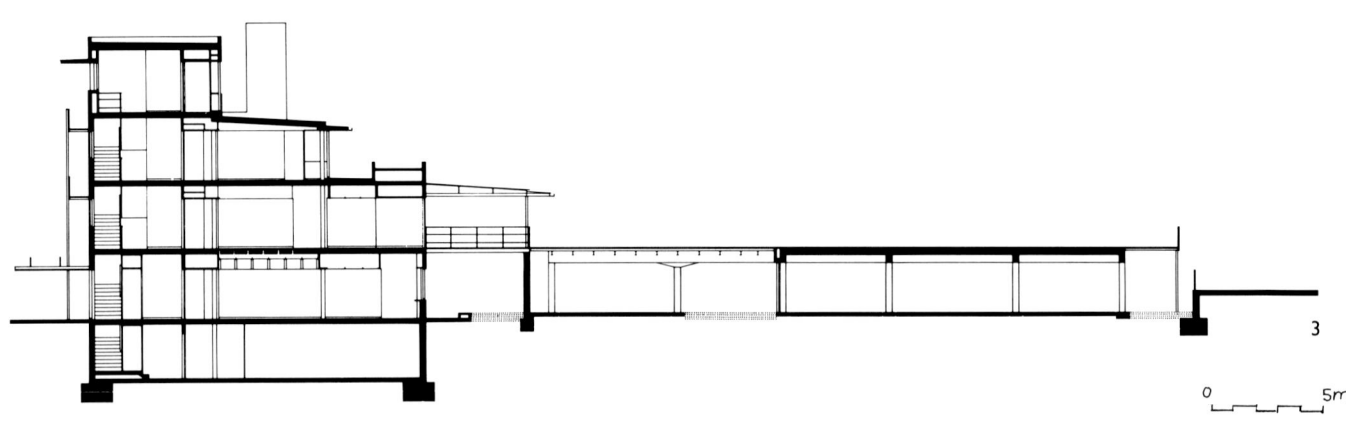

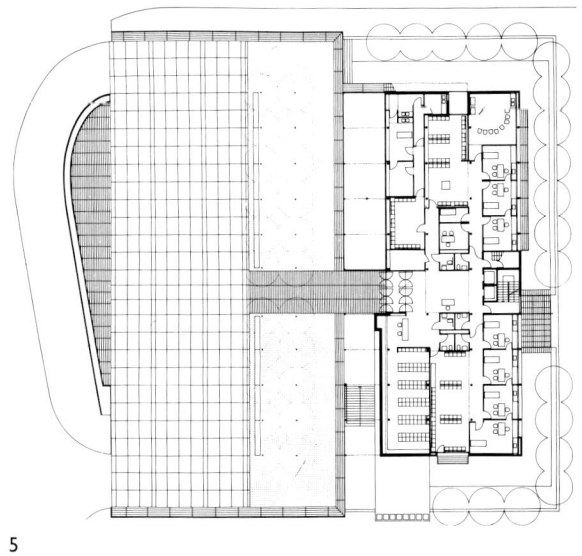
5

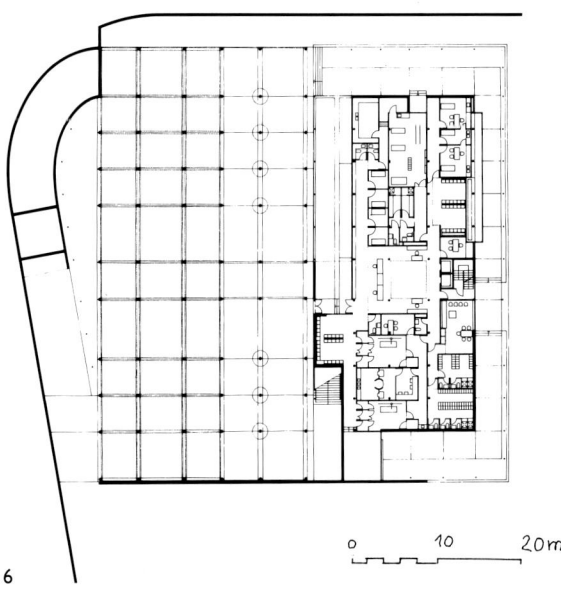
6

7

1 South façade
2 Corridor on the floor beneath the platform

DEVELOPER INSALUD. Catalonian Regional Government
SURVEYOR Jaume Martí Almestoy
CONSTRUCTION COMPANY Dragados y Construcciones, s.a.

Vilaseca Municipal Library

Rambla de Catalunya s/n
Vilaseca, Tarragona
1985-1986

In this case, the design had to take into account two somewhat contradictory circumstances of equal importance: the existence of a high party wall on the south boundary of the site, and the location of the site at the end of an avenue (built on a dry riverbed running perpendicular to the sea), which established an axis the building had to respect.

If this axis were respected by placing a symmetrical building facing onto the avenue, this would mean leaving the party wall intact and giving a rather unsatisfactory unfinished look to the whole, since the small surface area of the library (800 m^2) meant the building would be spread out horizontally rather than upwards, and would not be able to offset the high party wall by its volume. However, if the building were set right next to the wall, with access from the avenue, then the end of this important axis would be left hanging.

The problem was solved by locating the library building next to the party wall, but placing the access and the main façade overlooking a space created to prolong the avenue axis, marking its end whilst also providing a closed-off non-transit area that would be landscaped to establish the kind of silent, peaceful atmosphere that libraries seem to require.

This tree-lined space successfully continued the axis line established by the avenue. The party wall was then "put to use" to bear the load of the library building, continuity being guaranteed by the brick-colored tiles on the roof wall and on the library façade.

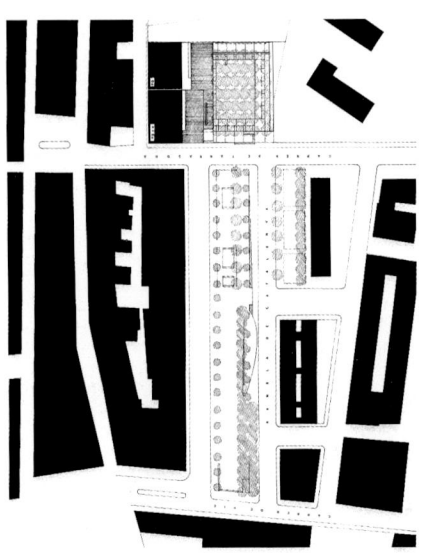

Area map
Double volume access space

Interior views of conference room

1 Northwest façade
2 Roof plan
3 First floor plan
4 Library entrance
5 Ground floor plan
6 Cross section
7 Entrance detail

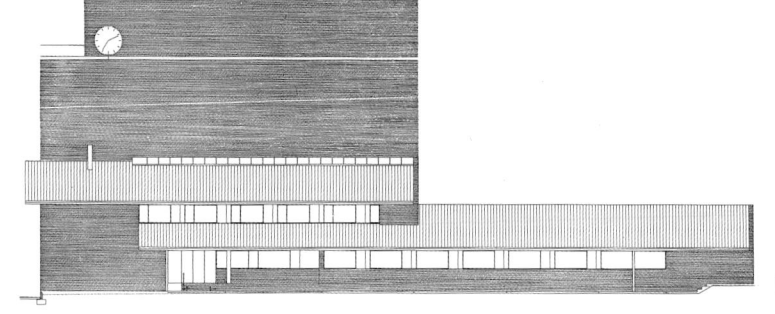

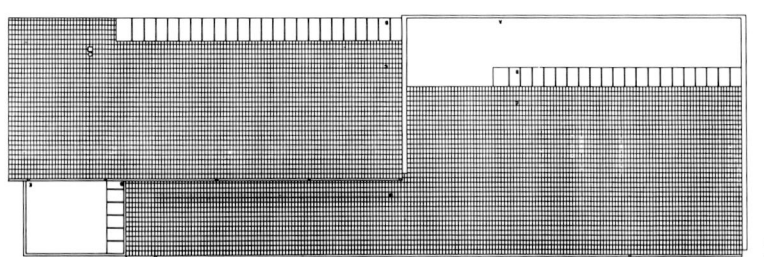

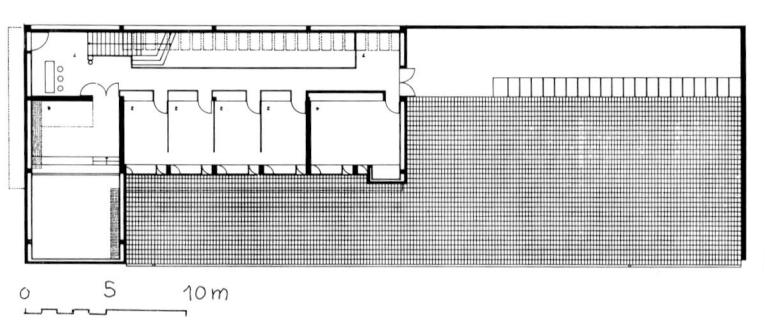

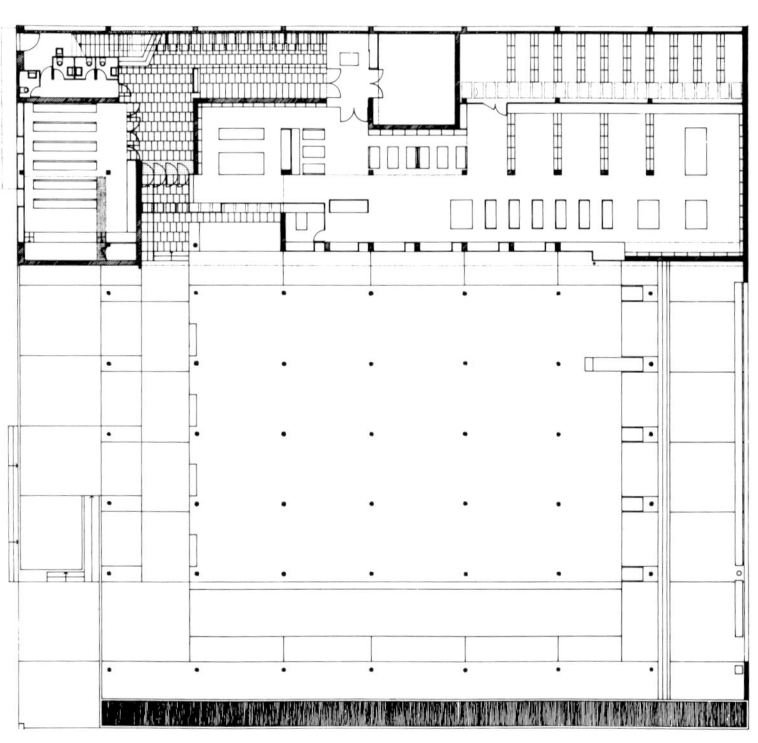

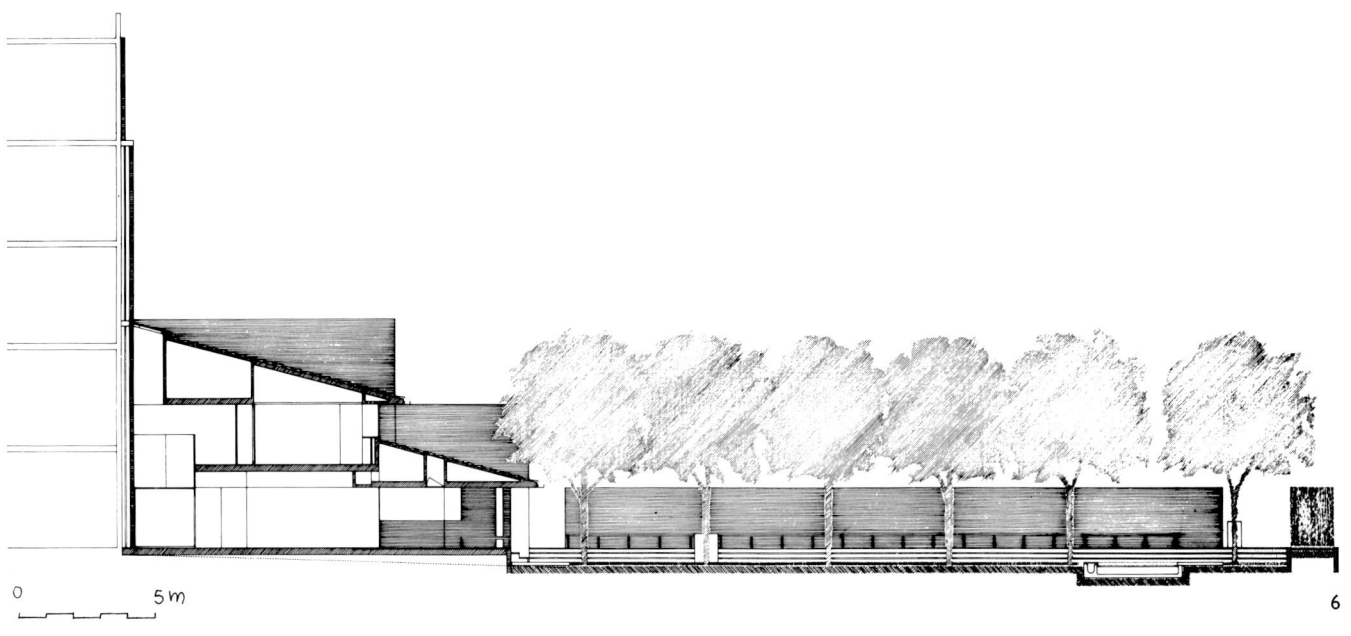

1 and 2 Interior views of reading room
3 Access to conference room amphitheater on the first floor

DEVELOPER Vilaseca Town Council
SURVEYOR Jaume Martí Almestoy
CONSTRUCTION COMPANY Servicios y Obras, s.a.

3

Detached House
Vidal i Ribas 34
Sant Feliú de Llobregat, Barcelona
1986-1988

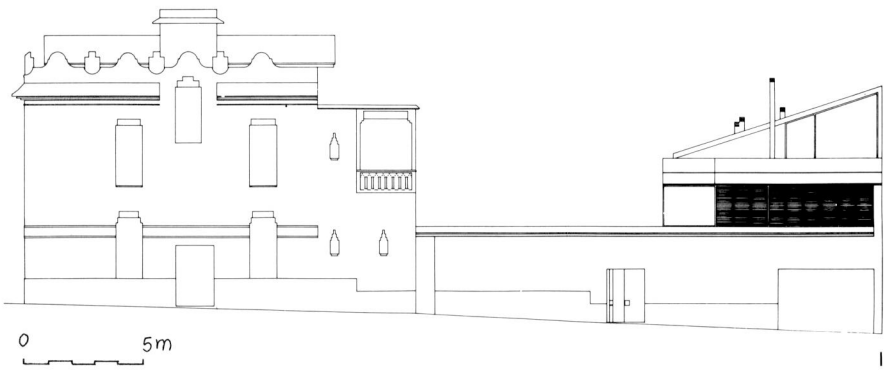

1 Elevation from Calle Vidal i Ribas
2 Area map
3 Entrance through shared courtyard

To a large degree, this house is the logical consequence of its surroundings. Located at the end of a row of modest houses, 4.5 m. wide, it stands next to a garden that was to be used jointly by this house and another much roomier one with an imposing façade, owned by the family, which had been built at the beginning of the century. While the size of the site and its position relative to the street and to the rear courtyard would seem to suggest a house in keeping with the adjoining terraced houses, the existence of a third façade overlooking the shared garden turns it into a unique building. On the one hand, it rounds off or terminates the row of houses, whilst on the other, it looks up to and offsets the big family house. This dependency was consolidated during the design stage, when the street façade disappeared as an active presence, ensconced behind a wall, the prolongation of which enclosed the garden and the big family house.

The design used the party wall to support the back of the house, and the roof was designed to accentuate this. A doorway opened in the wall provides access to the entrance, and from there to the interior of the house. The entrance is located in its center, marking a pleasant break between the street, or the public domain, and the entrance to the house, or the private domain.

The four vertical planes that make up the house are constituted differently according to their orientation, the constraints of the adjoining space and their use.

To the east, overlooking a small, landscaped courtyard, which has been artificially built up to lie at the level of the first floor, are the bedrooms. They look out directly onto the semi-private courtyard through tall windows reaching down to the floor.

To the north, jutting out from the façade over the garden, is the kitchen and laundry room, opening onto a generously proportioned gallery, which absorbs light and sun from the east and the west. It also provides a lookout point over the street entrance and establishes practical communication with the rear courtyard.

To the west, the dining room and living room look towards the street out over the extended garden wall, through a gallery that occupies the entire façade and which also functions as a bridge between the parallelepiped shape of the house and the wall that encloses the garden. Finally, the last room, an internal room without windows, is lit by a light shaft that illuminates the center of the house and establishes two-way ventilation for some of the rooms there.

1 Longitudinal section
2 Ground floor plan
3 First floor plan
4 Loft floor plan
5 North façade
6 Elevation from shared courtyard

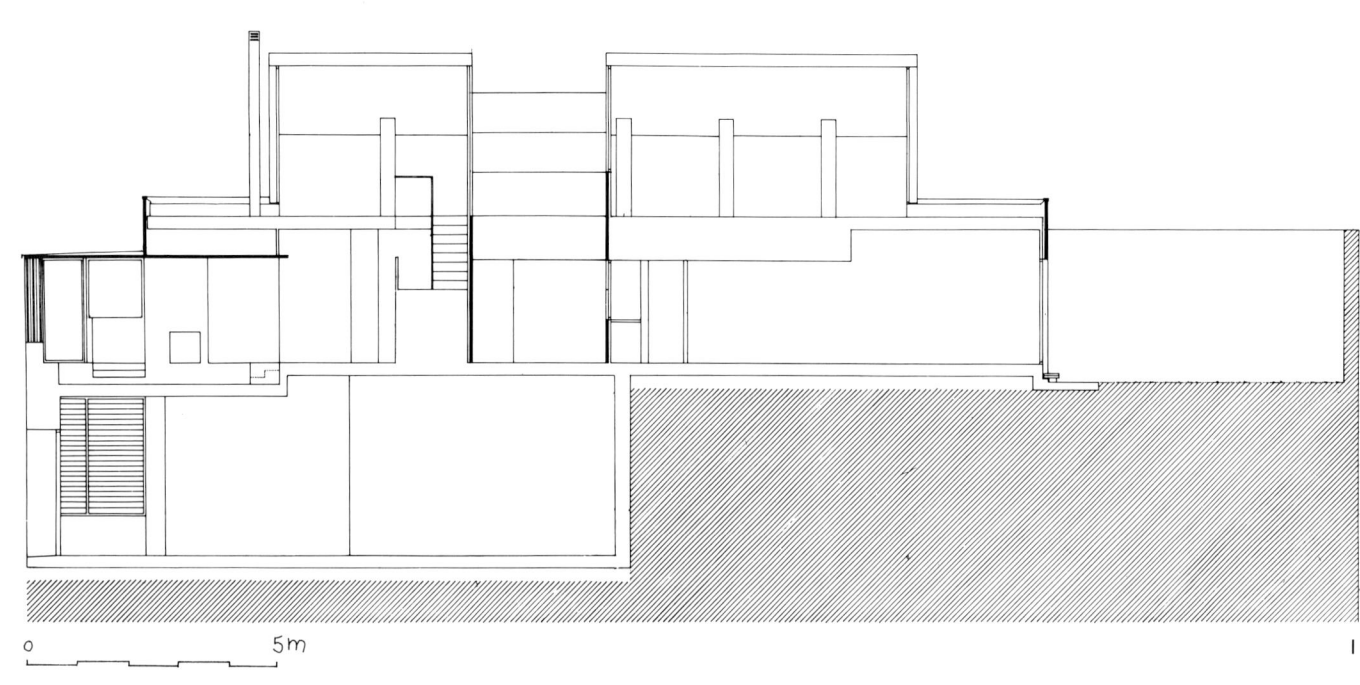

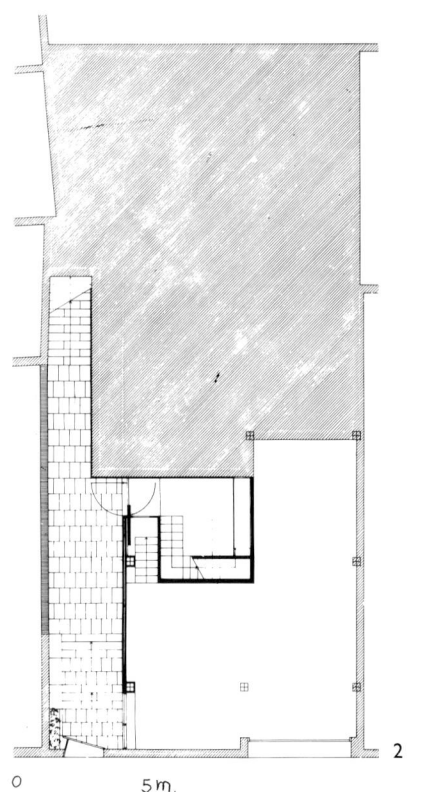
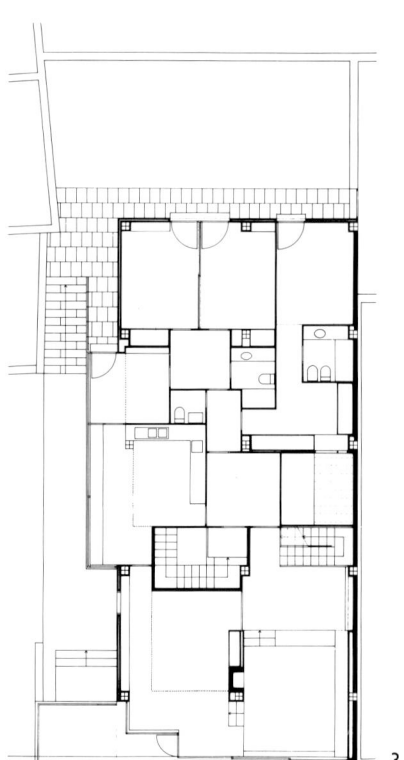
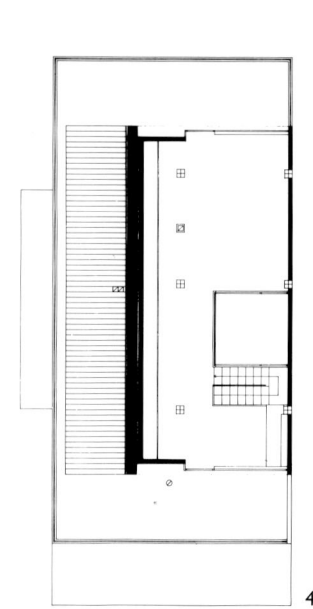

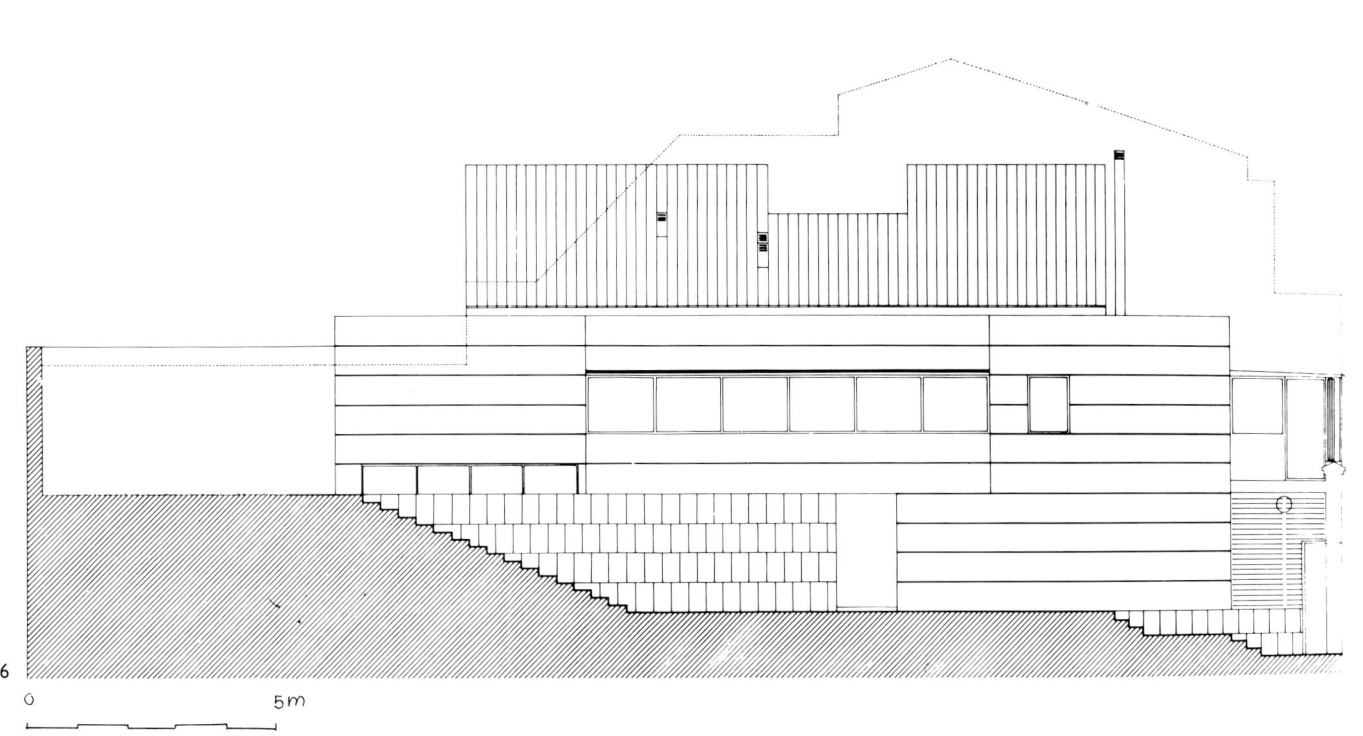

5

6

0   5m

1 House entrance from courtyard
2 Dining and living room
3 Cross section
4 North façade

2

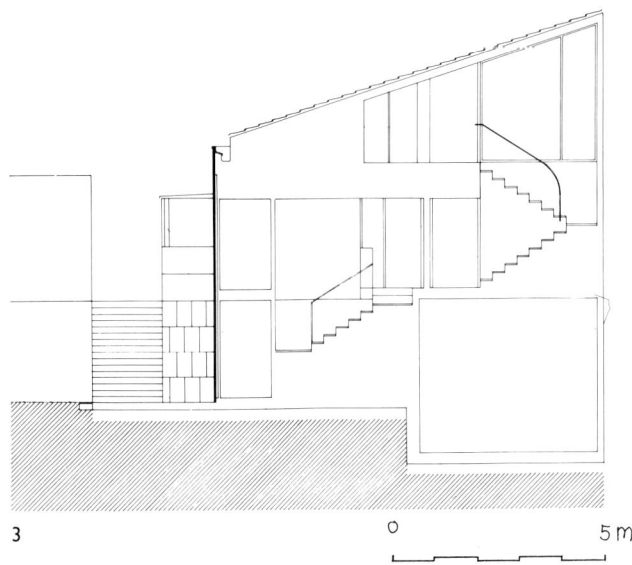
3

4

43

1 West façade and kitchen exit
2 First floor hall
3 Stairs to loft

2

3

OWNER Antoni Cahué
SURVEYOR Jaume Martí Almestoy
CONSTRUCTION COMPANY P. Tomás, s.a.

Refurbishment of the Barcelona Archaeological Museum
Paseo Santa Madrona 39-41
Barcelona
1984-1989

The Barcelona Archaeological Museum is housed in the building that was originally designed as the Palace of Graphic Arts for the International Exposition held in Barcelona in 1929.

The building is set out around a hexagon. Two pairs of differently sized bays symmetrically flank the entrance. Another pair of bays, and a large courtyard, are located on the same symmetrical axis on the side opposite the entrance.

The exterior treatment of the building concentrates almost exclusively on the entrance façade, where two porticos have been placed symmetrically to the entrance, in which the use of elements with obviously classical overtones is evident.

The capacity to assimilate changes whilst still maintaining a clearcut, strong formal structure is the most valuable aspect of this architecture, while the overbearingly large hexagon (albeit understandable if one thinks how much an ephemeral building in an Exposition needs to impress visitors) is its least interesting aspect.

The construction of the roofs, both for the bays and the central hexagon itself, is of special interest. It is a clearly ordered system, finished off in wood, which manages to endow the space it covers with meaning and scale.

In 1932, it was decided that the Barcelona Archaeological Museum should be housed here. Given the large surface area and volume available in the building, the first

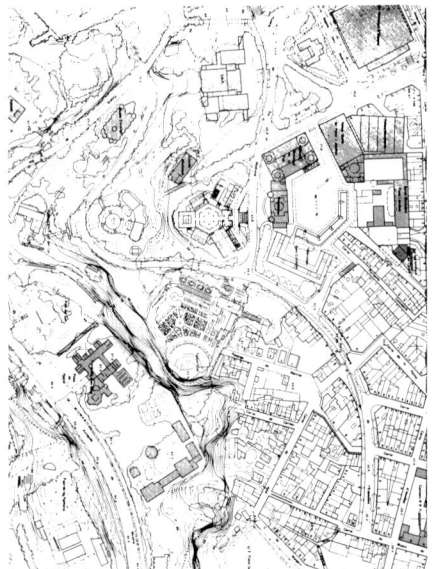

Area map
Central core. Ground floor

1 Section of building when work began
2 Proposed section
3 Mezzanine floor
4 Ground floor

round of refurbishing work was focused only on the largest bays and the central hexagon, as if another building were being constructed within the original structure.

Slab infill ceilings and walls were put in to hide the building's initial morphology. For example, the central hexagon and the ensuing geometry of the layout were ignored in order to divide the space up along orthogonal lines.

The general refurbishment began in 1935 and was followed by less comprehensive overhauls in 1940 and 1945, carried out with the same philosophy as the first one: using spaces that had been intended to show off the original structure and introducing low false ceilings and dividing walls that undermined the powerful scale of the Exposition building. Later on, small extension, conservation and repair works were done, normally with very tight budget constraints.

Thus, any visit to the museum was basically structured around the exhibition cases and dividing walls, which totally failed to take into account the scale of reference of the whole space, hiding it behind false ceilings and partition walls, so that it felt like a maze.

The public part of the museum had no natural light and no relationship with the outside, a waste in such a magnificent setting. Meanwhile, the museum services (administration offices, library, restoration workshop and part of the storerooms) were located on the first floor and looked like a makeshift solution which had become permanent by dint of time alone. One especially blatant case was the use of the museum director's apartment as a storeroom. It was also dysfunctional to have the weight of the storage on a first floor, with all the problems that moving pieces up and down for exhibition entailed.

The new design proposed recovering the original building, with its morphological structure, layout and building systems. This was to be done not only in accordance with its architectural values, but also, and above all, with its organizational capacities, using its structure to bring in a scale that would make it more than just a place where objects were displayed, turning it into a coherent exhibition space articulated around a single common element, the central hexagon.

Attention was to be focused on:

A. Locating the public display area on the first floor, reserving the ground floor for services and ancillary areas: the library, restoration workshop, administration offices and storerooms. In this way, access to such services would become independent from the public access, and the roofing would be recovered as a source of light, as in the original design, making it possible for the windows to become elements breaking up the intensity of the display and allowing the eye to wander outside. The roofing would also be used to provide a coherent structure uniting the diversity of exhibition spaces.

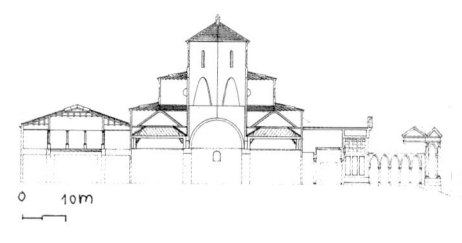
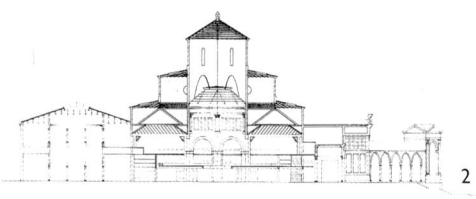
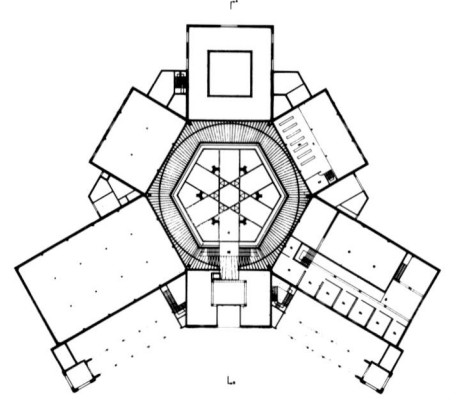
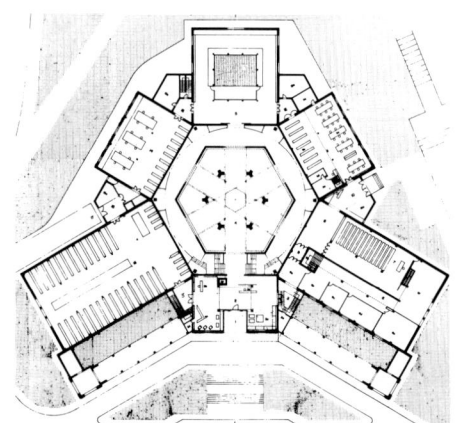

5 Ground floor
6 Ground floor. Flooring
7 Ground floor. Ceilings
8 Mezzanine floor
9 First floor. Flooring
10 First floor. Ceilings

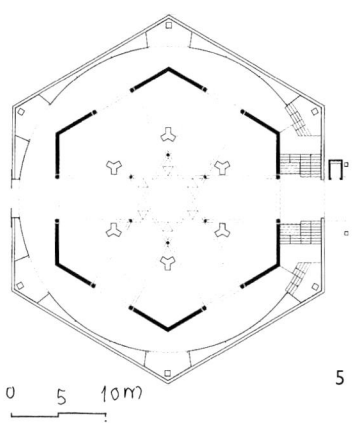

5

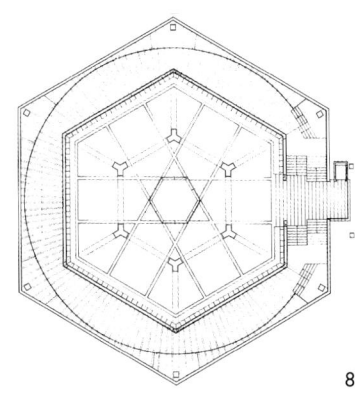

8

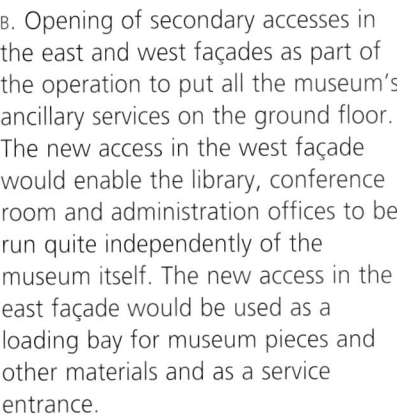

B. Opening of secondary accesses in the east and west façades as part of the operation to put all the museum's ancillary services on the ground floor. The new access in the west façade would enable the library, conference room and administration offices to be run quite independently of the museum itself. The new access in the east façade would be used as a loading bay for museum pieces and other materials and as a service entrance.

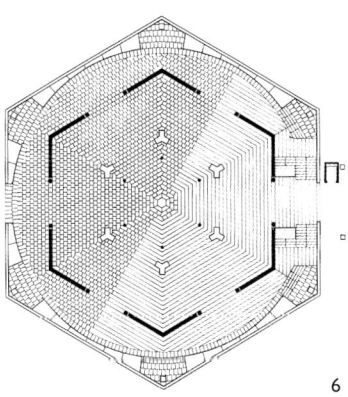

6

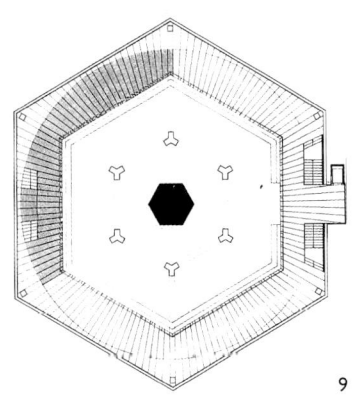

9

c. Reconstruction of the courtyard in the bay on the entrance axis, previously propped up by four pillars at the corners. It was proposed to leave the first foor of this bay covered but open at the sides, like a cloister, to make more room for pieces that could be displayed outside. The possibility of recovering the view of the courtyard or cloister on the first floor, from the moment of entering the building, seemed good for the entire building, since it would bring the Montjuïc gardens "inside" and also emphasize the hierarchical symmetry of the axis in the polydirectional hexagonal layout.

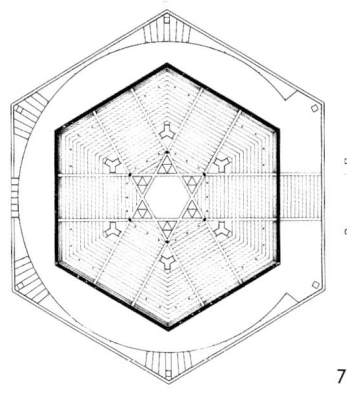

7

10

D. Re-using the central area of the hexagonal floor plan as a key space in the museum, as distributor and concourse for the entire building. This was the first part of the museum to be reformed, and the photographs of the final outcome belong to this area.

Visitors to the museum are ushered into this space on arrival, as the only access from the first floor and entrance to the five exhibition halls.

49

1 Ground floor passage
2 Central opening
3 Mezzanine and first floor

A new framework construction has been built, divided into two levels. The upper one is on the same level as the floor of the first storey of the bays, and acts as an access ring to the bays. The other one is at mezzanine level, to take advantage of part of the surface area of this central core which, if its totality were used for access to the bays, would be excessive. The ground floor, like the mezzanine, is a cul-de-sac, with stairs at the beginning to take visitors up to the first floor.

The bearing structure of all this new framework construction was designed independently from the original, and has created a new hexagon, smaller than the original one, which allows part of the hall to be used as more exhibition space. To avoid the different-sized parallel structures being too obvious, the ground floor hexagon has been covered with a circular wooden screen.

3

1 Circular showcase on the ground floor
2 Staircase from ground to first floor

2

DEVELOPER Barcelona Provincial Council
SURVEYOR Jaume Martí Almestoy
CONSTRUCTION COMPANY Fomento de Obras y Construcciones, s.a.

Engineering School Library, Lecture Rooms and Departments
Escuela de Ingenieros de Caminos. Universidad Politécnica de Barcelona
Campus Nord, Barcelona
1987–1989

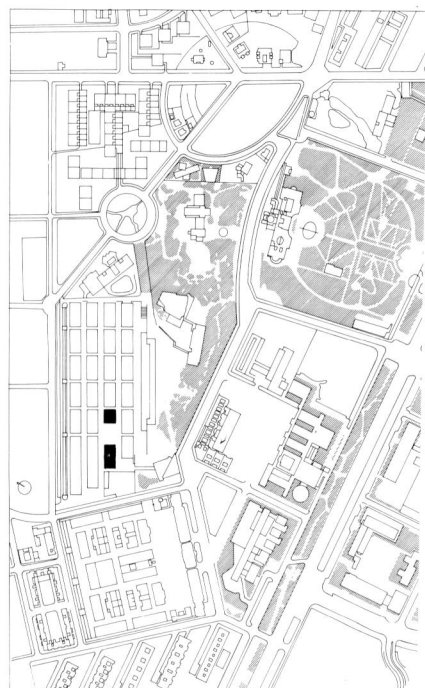

Area map
Library and department buildings

This building, one of many on the extensive Universidad Politécnica de Barcelona campus, is nonetheless unique. It is much smaller than its neighbours and one of its façades overlooks a space that is equally unique with regard to the pedestrian walkways that organize the entire layout.

The building reflects both circumstances and slots into its due place with docility, using similar materials to the neighboring blocks, maintaining alignment with them and aiming for neutrality, since it is subordination to the whole that is at a premium here. At the same time, it exploits the singularity of the wide, open space in front of its west façade, locating its entrances there through an element that acts not only as a canopy but also a stairway and a balcony. It is defined according to the basic specifications determining that the ground floor should be used for common services (bar, copy shop, etc.) and the first and second for teaching purposes (lecture and seminar rooms, library, etc.).

Given the small surface area available for the library, compared to the meters of shelving required, it was decided not to have windows onto the exterior, except for the library staff rooms, and to light it with an overhead system letting in the diffuse natural light from the north and small 10-centimeter openings that let in the more lively, changing sunlight.

At the same time, designing began for a second building, for departmental use, of a similar size to the others in the campus. The changes in use and programming (which continued during the building stage) focused the design on the definition of how the building was to be enclosed. Thus, each of the façades was constructed with the same kinds of materials and elements as the other building (aluminum window frames on the outside, brick, etc.), whilst the specific conditions of orientation and position with relation to the walkways on the campus and the roads outside it were also taken into account. The longer north and south façades were set back below the first floor in order to provide a larger section for the walkways. To the south, this was done by forming a running balcony, where students could go out from the teaching rooms between classes; and to the north, by making a gallery that gives views in the direction parallel to the pedestrian street. The gallery then runs along the first and second storeys of the east façade, in order to establish a direct visual relationship between the inside of the building and the public space outside it. To the west, the same gallery was decorated with slat blinds to shut out the setting sun, and with a small attic, which seems to set off the building to perfection (the last in the second row), like a small red lighthouse, giving this face of the block the urban dimension required to connect it with the built-up landscape of the street that bounds the campus on this side.

The balconies and galleries in this building are also instruments for setting back the façades as the storeys rise. In this way, the volume of the building is reduced and the walkways are not dwarfed by solid planes of building above them.

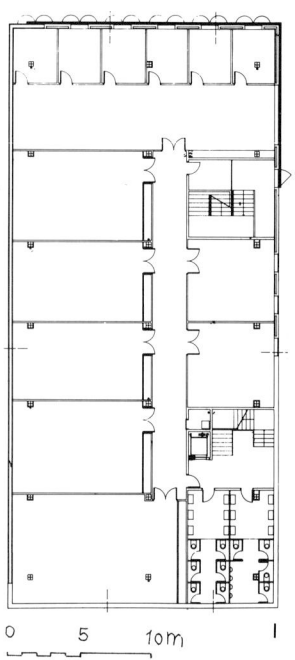
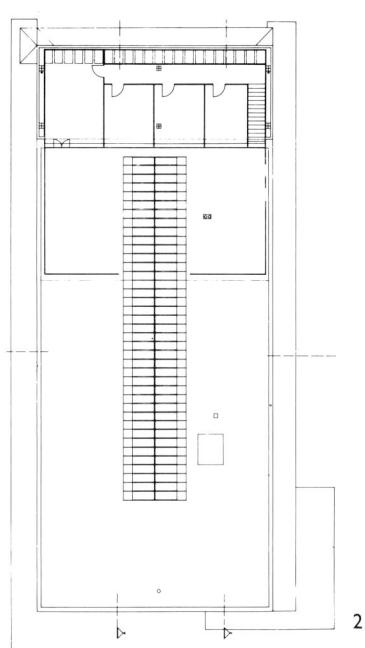
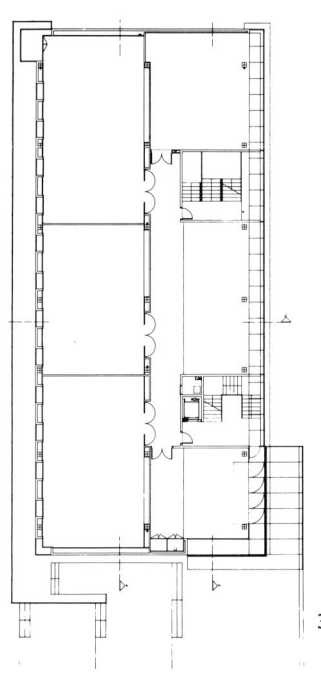

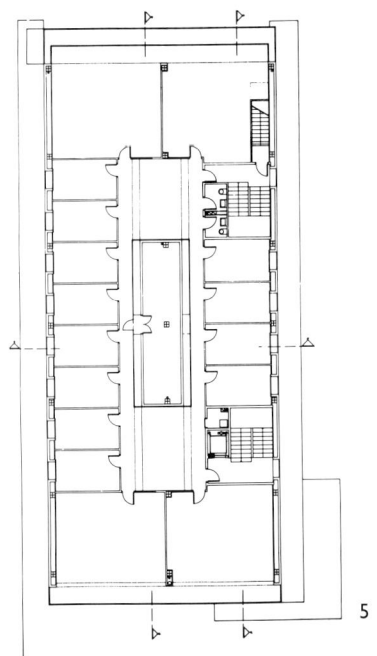
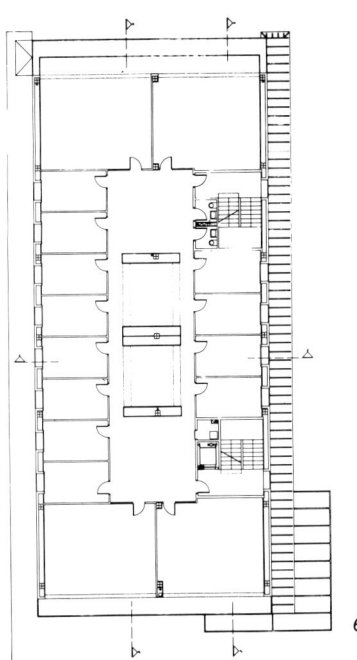

1, 2, 3, 5 and 6 Floor plans
4 Northwest façade
7 Southwest façade

1 Exterior staircase to library
2 Cross section
3, 4 and 5 Floor plans
Overleaf: library reading room

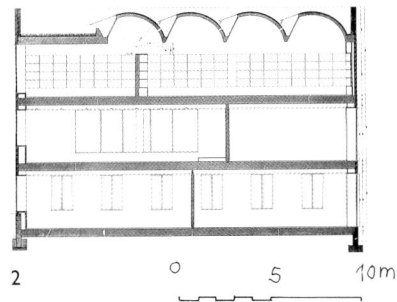

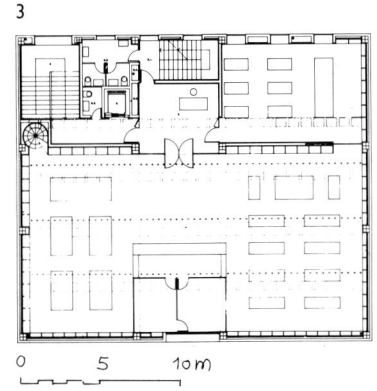

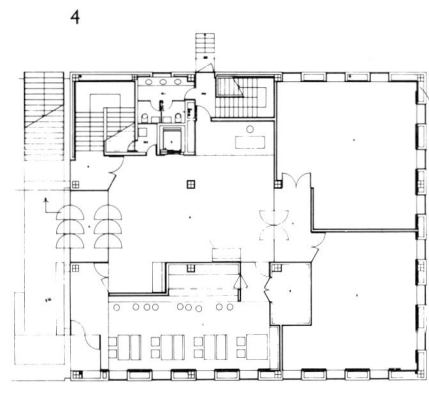

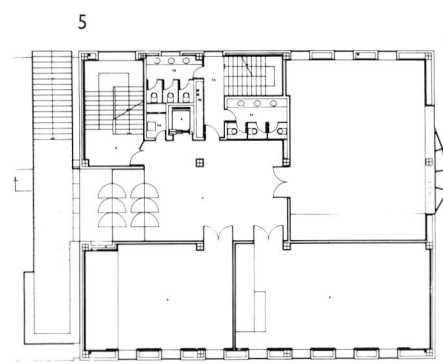

1 Library. Main façade
2 Department building. Southeast corner
3 Library. South façade

DEVELOPER Universidad Politécnica de Barcelona
SURVEYOR Jaume Martí Almestoy
CONSTRUCTION COMPANY Deco, s.a.

Office and Apartment Building
Avenida de Tarragona 35
Vilafranca del Penedés, Barcelona
1988-1990

The disproportionate dimensions of the site (5.2 x 27.38 m.) were further aggravated by the imposition of a statutory height limit of 16.50 m. The façades thus vary enormously in size (5.20 x 16.5 and 27.38 x 16.5 m.) and also overlook quite different kinds of roads. The 5.2-meter-wide façade on Avenida de Tarragona looks onto one of the key urban thoroughfares in Vilafranca, whilst the 27.38-meter-wide façade over Calle Bisbe Morgades gives onto a narrow secondary street, of the kind so typical in Vilafranca.

On the side opposite Bisbe Morgades, the site borders an early-twentieth-century three-storey building, which is listed for conservation under the General Town Plan. The relationship with this building, the disproportionate dimensions of the new building and the importance of the node that connects Calle Bisbe Morgades and Avenida de Tarragona as the point of articulation between two very different kinds of street were issues of potential conflict that the design had to overcome.

The solution to the problem of establishing the relationship with the existing building was found not on the façade over Avenida Tarragona but on the façade perpendicular to Calle Bisbe Morgades, especially on the two top floors. These will always loom higher than the listed building, but the peculiar proportions were resolved by hiding the fourth floor behind the roof. The issue of being a wedge between streets was dealt with by bringing in a small gallery on the corner, slightly out of line with the rest of the ground plan.

1 Area map
2 Relationship between existing building and new building
3 Rear façade

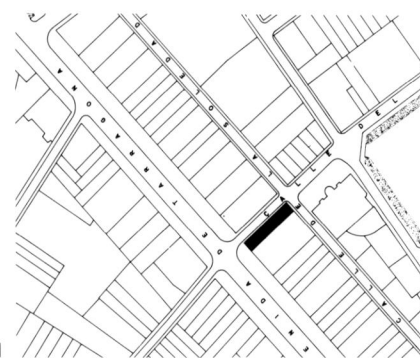

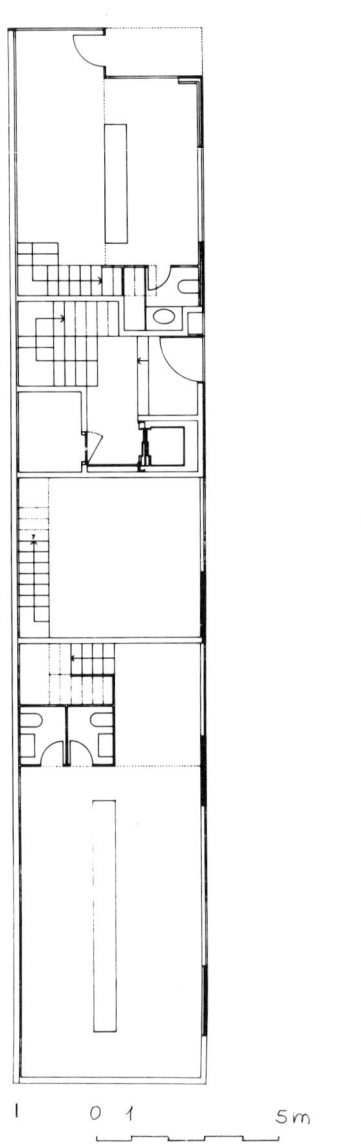
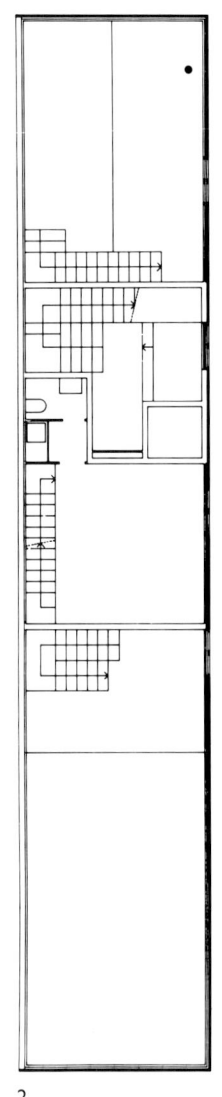
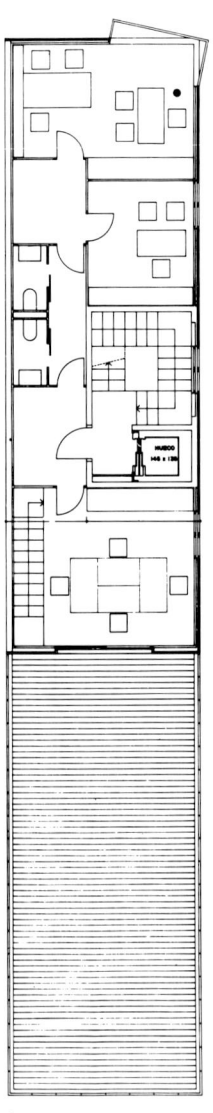
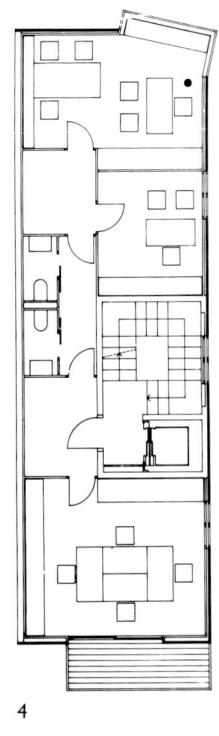

1 to 8 Floor plans
9 Rear façade
10 Main façade

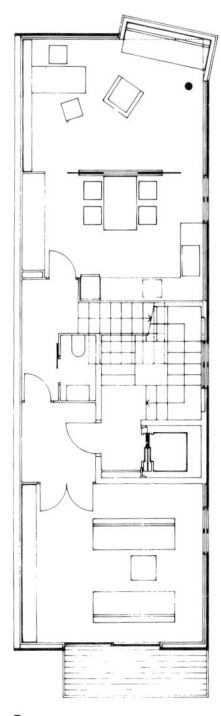

5

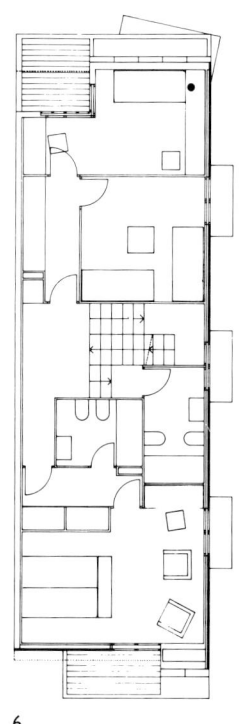

6

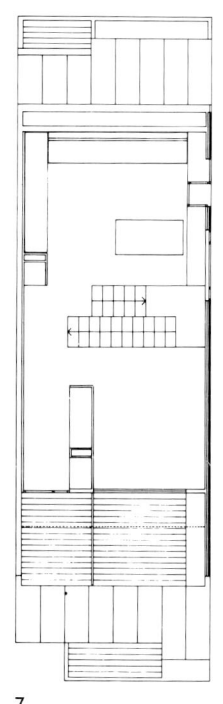

7

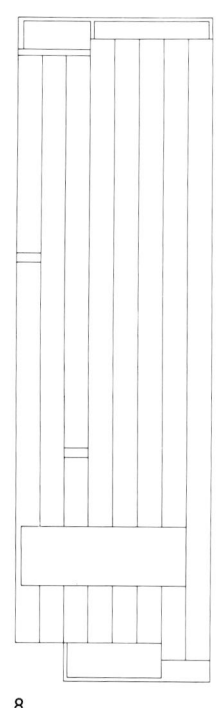

8

OWNER José Ballester
SURVEYOR Jaume Martí Almestoy
CONSTRUCTION COMPANY Josep Salat, s.a.

10

Apartment Building in Vallcarca

Sant Eudald 16-18
Barcelona
1991-1996

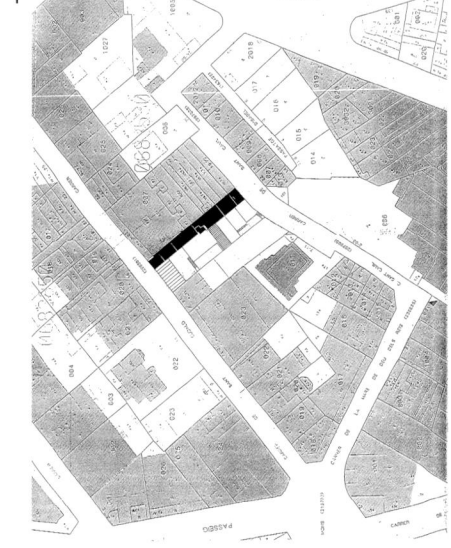

1 Area map
2 Street façade
3 Decorative tower

The site was highly asymmetrical. An enormous residential block towering over one side of it, the result of now outdated town planning regulations, left a party (lotline) wall to the east. To the west, a low-rise house between two party walls, a common kind of building in the neighborhood, set off this difference in height.

The site was also extremely raked, with a 12 m. drop from one street to the next. These factors led to the initial design of four separate houses forming a 4 m. corridor, as high and as wide as possible, lining the party wall, with small perpendicular annexes to form living rooms and access courtyards.

Just as building was about to begin, the owners changed their mind and the two highest apartments were turned into a single home for them. Later, the same was done to the other two, turning them into a second home with office space and a garage.

These transformations make the underlying order (initially four repetitions of a single unit) hard to discern and apparently arbitrary. However, the initial goals of the design were maintained: to construct a narrow corridor (now 4.5 m.) attached to the neighboring party wall.

1 Perspective of initial design
2 Final design
3 to 10 Floor plans
11 Façade onto access courtyard
Overleaf: view from terrace

1

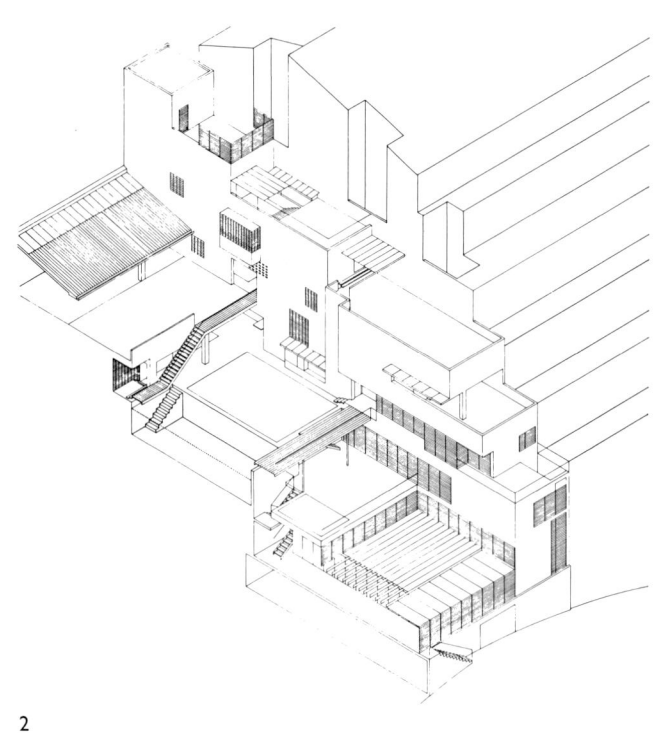

2

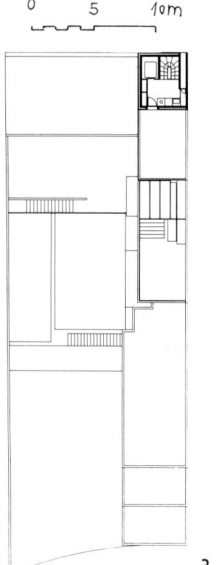

3

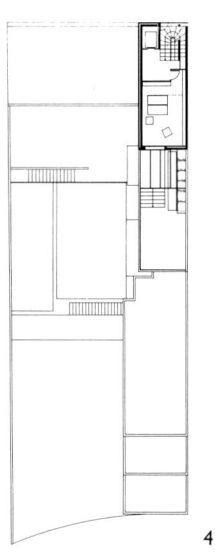

4

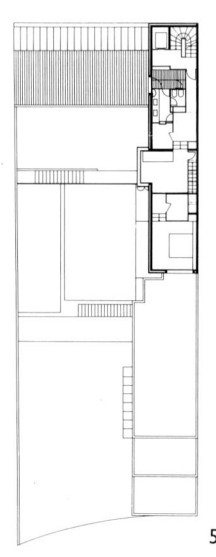

5

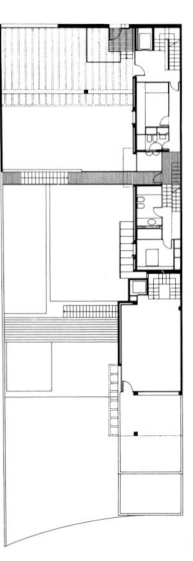

6

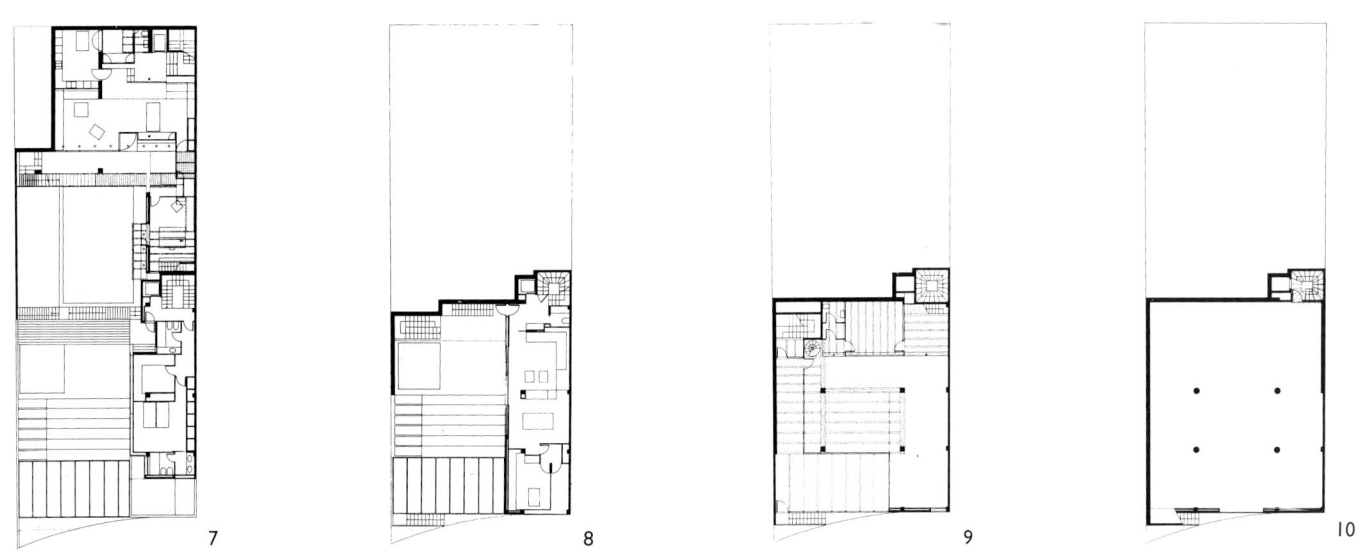

7
8
9
10

71

1 Living room
2 Stairway from living room
3 Handrail detail

OWNER Pedro Sala
SURVEYOR Jaume Martí Almestoy
CONSTRUCTION COMPANY Catalana d'Obres, s.a.

Detached House in Can Caralleu

Capella de Can Caralleu 12
Barcelona
1991-1993

Area map
Interior terrace from kitchen

Can Caralleu lies at the foot of Collcerola. Originally consisting of houses put up by their owners without relationship to Barcelona, the neighborhood was gradually linked to the city network as it grew.

The site is on a steep south-facing slope with marvelous views of the city. It covers some thousand square meters, has access from two streets (with a 14 m. drop between the two), and is set in a densely built-up neighborhood.

The house is located on the mid level, cornered in and set against the back of the land in order to obtain the largest terrace possible, stretching the living room, the dining room and even the kitchen outwards.

There is still some unresolved indecision between the house as a parallelepiped, as an independent box in the middle of the mountains, and the house as an excavation in the ground, as a cave or refuge.

This lack of clarity in the design is largely due to the lack of specific planning regulations. The rules that say it must be 3 m. away from the neighbors – i.e., an isolated house – are impossible to keep on such steep slopes, since the enormous drops make it inevitable that the site be terraced with supporting walls connecting the house to the shared boundaries.

The result is a house set apart but also linked to the neighboring ones by the outer walls.

During building, there were substantial changes of plan. Budget constraints eliminated the entrance to the garage from the lower street and various outer walls in the lower half of the site. It was then decided to raise the roof of the second floor some 50 cm. to make a flat area on which to park, with access from the upper street. This meant the access to the house, originally planned through the ground floor from the garage, also needed changing, and required improvising another entrance at the back of the house through the bedroom floor.

The new access from the flat roof was via stairs against a wall running down to the ground floor in six syncopated zigzags. Thus, the ground floor is left as a large unbroken surface, extending through the windows onto the terrace, with a beautiful view of the city and Montjuïc.

"At times, the owner would have wished we had managed to deviate the stark stare of the building materials; introducing into the house the slight smile with which Tessenow referred to decoration; extracting from the long hours of cumulative work on the materials the scattered, fleeting reflections of night-time rest..."

J. Llinás

1 to 3 Floor plans
4 Access from upper street

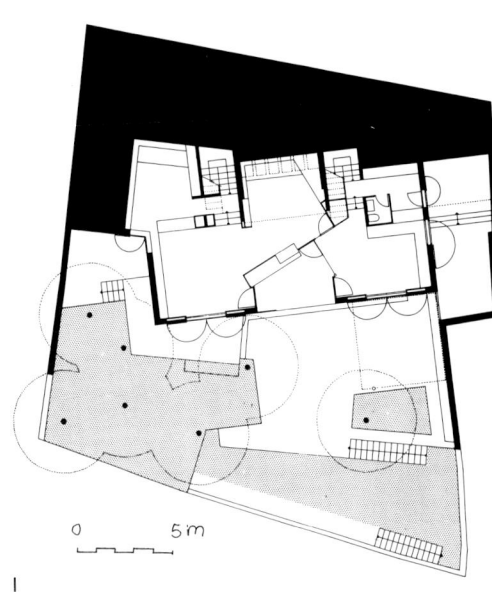

1

4

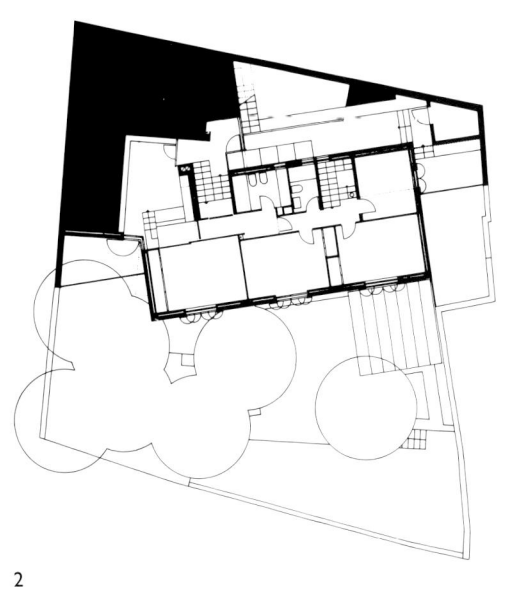

2

3

1 Access courtyard
2 Axonometric projection of initial design
3 Axonometric projection of executed design

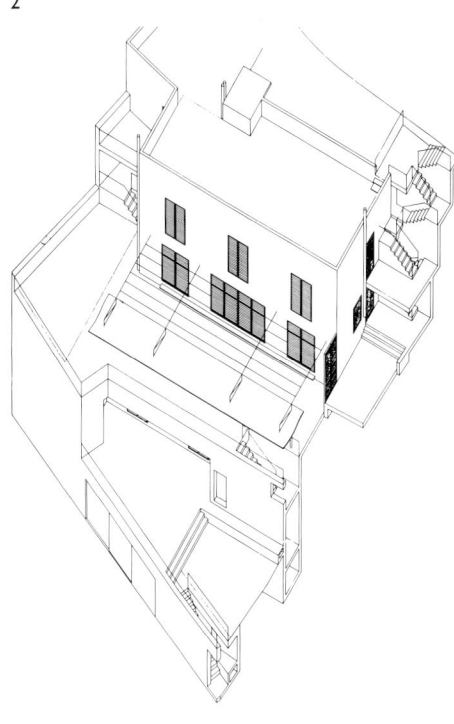

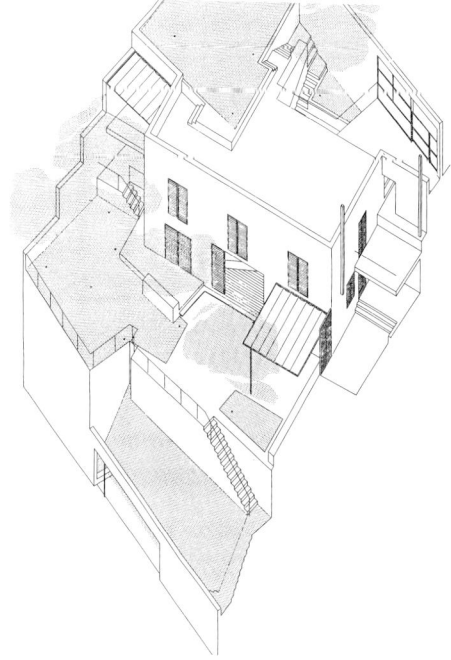

1

2

1 Access to house interior
2 Hall
3 Stairway to living room
4 Study and main bedroom as seen from the staircase

1 Living-dining room
2 South façade
3 Terrace joining kitchen, dining room and living room

1

OWNER Enric Company – Milagros Pérez-Oliva
SURVEYOR Jaume Martí Almestoy
CONSTRUCTION COMPANY Pedro Asensio, s.a.

Detached House in Colonia Güell
Claudio Güell 18
Santa Coloma de Cervelló, Barcelona
1991-1994

Problems with the Administration meant this was a long drawn-out job. This, however, allowed the design to take its time, slowly adapting itself to the peculiar scale of the Colonia Güell residential estate.

Basically, the economy with which the modest buildings of the estate were built also affected measurements: ceiling heights of 2.30 m., doors and windows in proportion, but "shrunk," etc. The drawing, showing a house with conventional measurements, is proof of this.

Consequently, it was decided that in order to fit into the estate, the building would have to be shrunk without turning it into a caricature, increasing some measurements while reducing others.

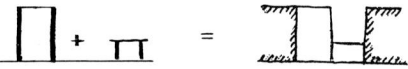

The garage, the door to the garage, looked too different from the other neighboring houses. This problem was solved by breaking up the building into a house plus a garage, avoiding tension between the two parts.

In the end, the drive access is probably too public and the use of the stairs on the façade a bit too striking for passersby. This staircase, however, was intentionally used to set the building apart from the neighboring house, making it clear how the party wall backs onto the building, while the other wall acts like a profile or section.

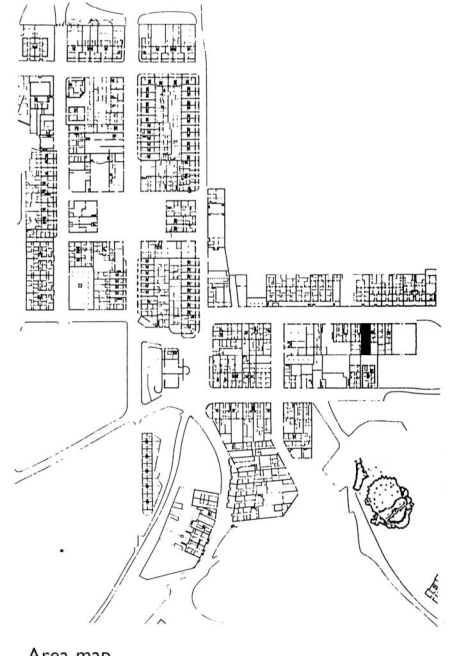

Area map
Garage on ground floor

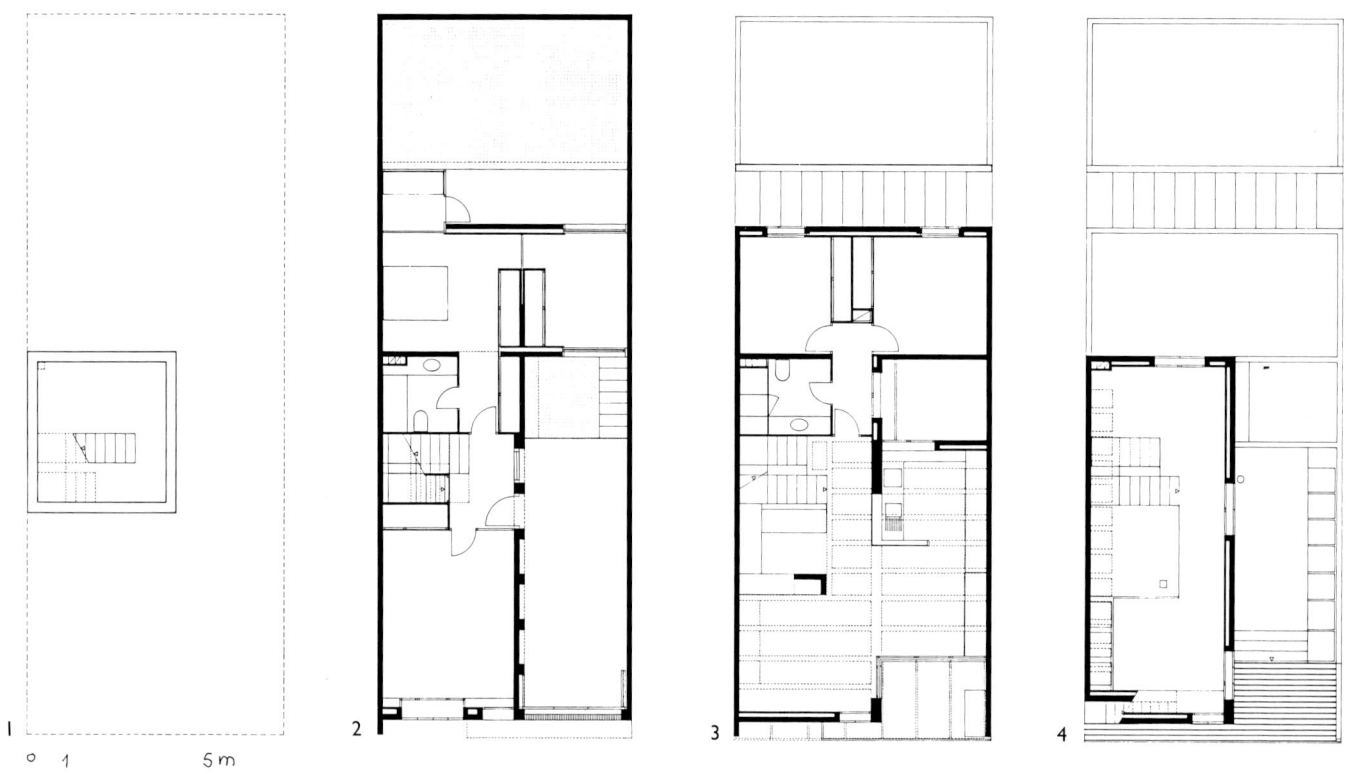

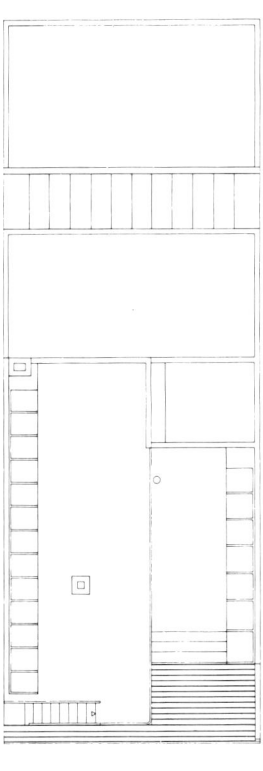

1 to 5 Floor plans
6 Living room
7 Street façade
8 Stairs and kitchen

1 and 2 Study on second floor

OWNERS Santi Maldonado-Luz Mínguez
SURVEYOR Jaume Martí Almestoy
CONSTRUCTION COMPANY Germans Font

Restoration of the Metropol Theater
Rambla Nova 46
Tarragona
1992-1995

The Patronat Obrer Theater (1908) was one of Josep María Jujol's first commissions as an independent architect.

As with most of his commissions, this one entailed modifying an existing building, which stood on a back street, Calle Armanyà. Here Jujol had to make a stage and then build the seating area for the public in the rear garden or courtyard. He also built a new gallery to provide access to the theater from Rambla Nova, crossing the ground floor of an existing block of housing.

It is important to note that the Rambla Nova access is one storey higher than the Calle Armanyà access. This means that the Rambla Nova entrance to the theater hall was located at the level of the dress circle.

The Patronat Obrer Theater, owned by the Diocese of Tarragona, was a modest building, designed to provide simple facilities for small performances, end-of-term parties or local institutional events linked to the Church.

Jujol never finished work on the theater due to misunderstandings with the Diocese (e.g., another professional was brought in to put the finishing touches on the proscenium). After he left, the building was subjected to a concatenation of indignities.

During the Spanish Civil War, several bombs fell on the gallery, which was later reconstructed using the original structure, but supporting it with another system and mutilating the woodwork. Years later, it was turned into the Metropol Cinema, which entailed closing it off from any light and putting in lavatories and other installations to meet safety standards. This was done with little respect for the original design, and when the cinema closed down in the Eighties, it was simply abandoned and soon fell into ruin.

In the end, the Tarragona City Council, at the request of several institutions including the Tarragona Professional College of Architects, purchased the building in order to turn it into a municipal theater.

As in so many of Jujol's works, the original theater had been built on a shoestring with whatever came to hand. For example, many of the windows for the dress and upper circles were recycled, so that they had little to do with the space onto which they opened. One of them was, in fact, a door that was simply laid horizontally.

Similarly, the ironwork columns supporting the gallery had nothing to do with the cross-shaped ones in the structure of the first floor of the gallery, which were definitely Jujol's design. They seem to have been brought in from elsewhere or perhaps from another structure that just happened to be in the courtyard where the theater was built.

There were nonstructural walls 10 cm. thick and the most unlikely type of structural walls imaginable, e.g., the staircase that goes down to the stalls area is supported on three V-shaped

Area map
The handrail on the stairs, at the rear in the photograph, is modeled on a sewing needle for fishing nets

1 Floor plan of upper circle when work began
2 Floor plan of dress circle (access from Rambla level) when work began
3 Floor plan of stalls level (floor -1 from Rambla level) when work began

walls, which get thinner as they move down to the vertex at the bottom, where they are only 10 cm. thick. The effect is beautiful, as are the results of many of Jujol's extremely heterodox building techniques.

Further, the woodwork enclosing the gallery was shifted at Jujol's own indication during the building work, so that the doors opened outwards and the balconies led inwards. One can only imagine that these changes were done to stop the open door leaves from obstructing people's movement. But these factors only complicated any attempt at remodeling yet further.

This was the starting point for the work executed from 1992 to 1995: a modest, heterodox building, bombed and then treated with a distinct lack of consideration, on the verge of collapse. From here it was necessary to go back to 1908 to rediscover the freshness of the original design.

This was all the information available. None of the original plans had survived. The graphic material at our disposal consisted of an amateur photograph of the theater hall and two or three drawings by people who had gone out of their way to record aspects of the theater's interior.

From what Jujol's son states in *Jujol, un artista completo*, it was also clear that the theater had been conceived as a religious allegory: a boat (the nave of a church) in which the spectators would embark to find refuge from the stormy seas of life.

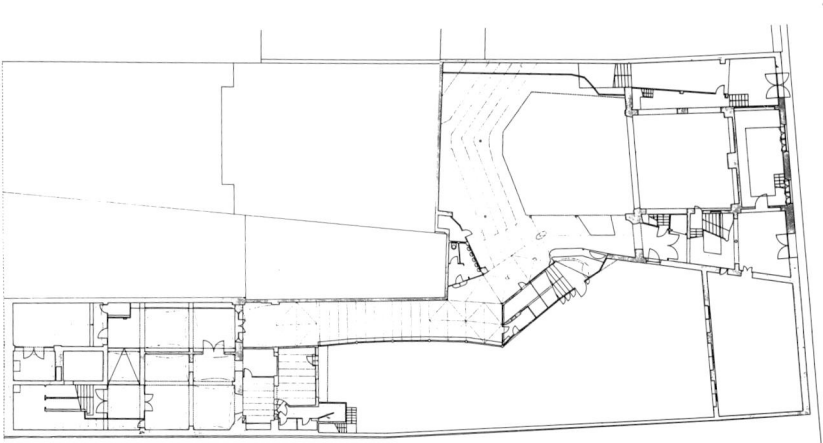

4 Blueprint plan of upper circle
5 Blueprint plan of upper circle
6 Blueprint plan of stalls

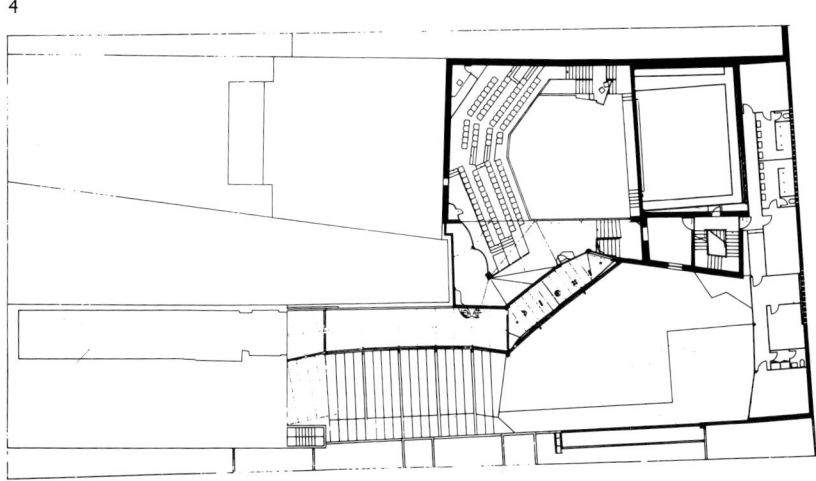

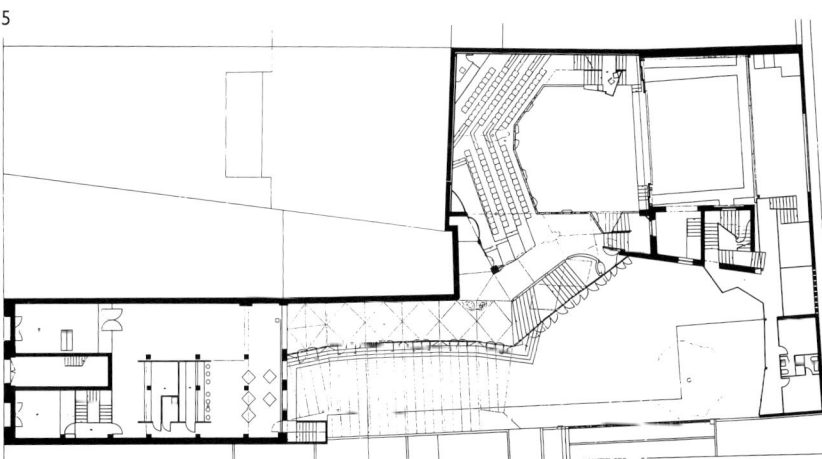

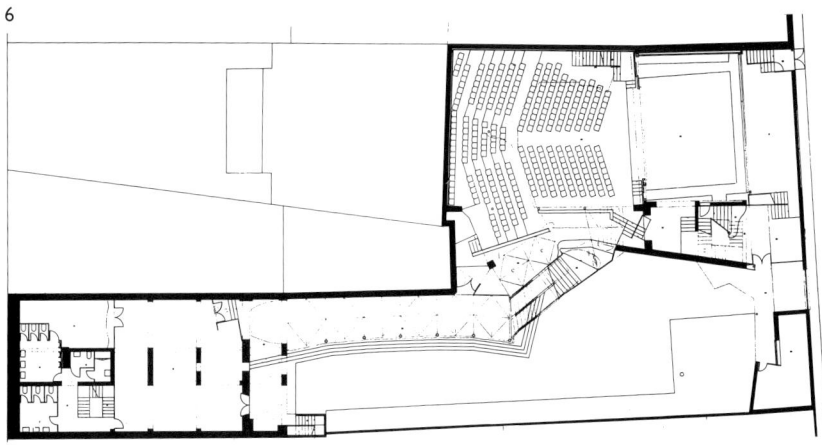

When we began analyzing the work, we saw that this idea of a boat or nave was not only an allegory, but also the compositional order governing the transformation of all the different elements of the building.

Moreover, while we were doing the design, we came to the conclusion that the hypothetical Plimsoll line was situated at the height of the gallery floor. Below this, everything was underwater.

Clues to this were:

– the whirlpools in the floor and the ceiling before the staircase going down to the stalls level.

– the drawings of waves and fish on the steps of the stairs as they go down, and the lines etched into the edge of the steps, similar to the lines that the tide makes on the sand.

– the way the staircase is supported on the three V-shaped brick walls, clearly making reference to the keel of a boat.

– the ceiling of the stalls, near the stairs, reminiscent of the surface of the sea as seen from below, when diving.

– the ceiling of the stalls-level gallery, which curves downward, with domes hanging like boat hulls.

– the solid brickwork pillar on the dress-circle level which is decorated with leaves and crowned "M's" (initial of Mary), while at stalls level, it has encrusted fish and sea snails.

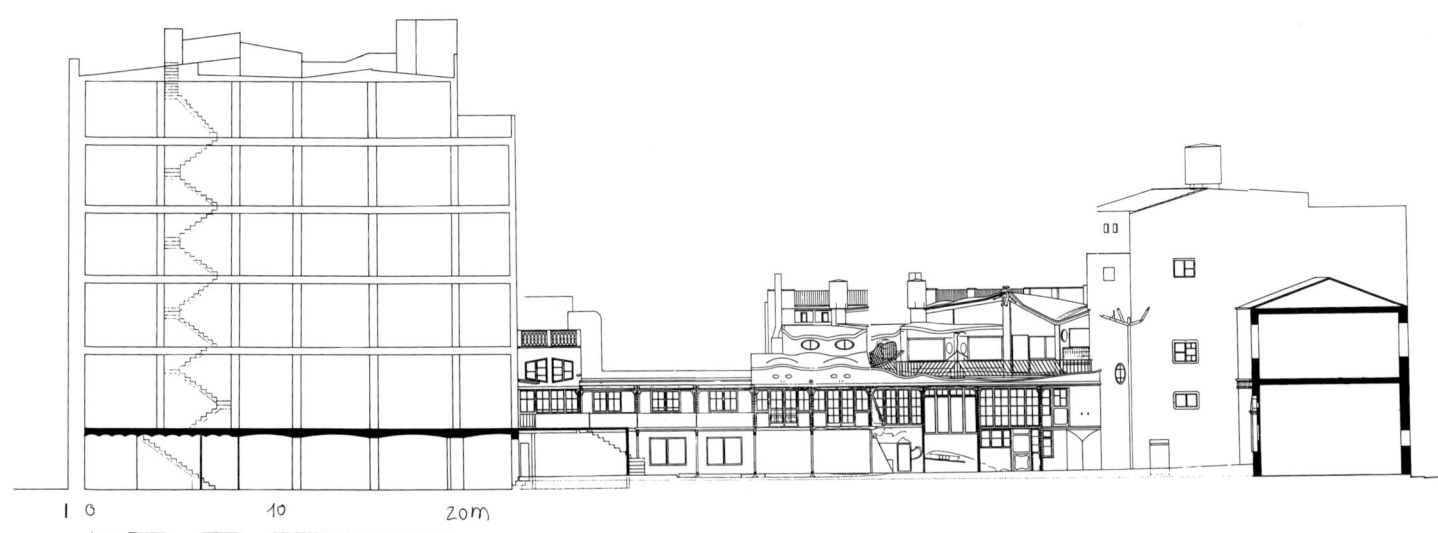

1 Longitudinal section through the courtyard when work began

– from the courtyard, the corner or articulation between the gallery and the staircase going down to the stalls, which was treated as a boat prow on purpose, using infills to accentuate its directionality from the perpendicular.

– the moulding on the finishing of the base of this wall, which either reproduced or was inspired by the effect of a boat moving over the water.

There was probably some truth in this interpretation, then, although Jujol did not impose it very rigidly: on the ceiling of the gallery of the stalls level, for example, there are etchings of seaweed and wavy lines (this is the underwater section), but also of stars, palm trees, a bat and some kind of lion.

What is certain is that the aquatic world, intermingling with the cult of the Virgin Mary, is what Josep María Jujol used to guide his building design in the theater.

The Metropol re-creates this private, rather special interpretation of water: the fish (another important symbol for early Christianity), foam, whirlpools, seaweed and sand all mixed together with the crowned M's; the word MARIA (Mary) engraved in the wood, the letters so far apart that they can only be read by those in the know; the crown of thorns over the water deposit, etc.

All this is further spiced up by two typically Jujolian components: the use of second-hand materials creating a relaxed tone (look at the meeting between the iron pillar and the bridging joist in the gallery "prow"), and Jujol's innate skill at injecting inert buildings with "spirit" (almost in the theological sense).

On the basis of these hastily described precedents, it becomes clear that the remodeling work required was complex, full of hesitation, and very varied. In brief:

A. NEW BUILDING WORK

The ground floor of the building giving onto Rambla Nova in which Jujol was never involved, was cleared of walls and accessory elements to form the theater hall. The space in the hall is defined almost exclusively by the existing load-bearing system in the building. All we did was use it to mark a grid of secondary girders and joists on the false ceiling, whose geometrical order is like a blank paper for spectators, the raw material that Jujol manipulated as an essential part of his style.

This attitude, maintaining the scale, the materials and even the modest nature of the Jujolian construction in the new parts, but evidently without his typical embossments, incisions and drawings, was our key to defining the set of dressing rooms that closes the theatre off on the Calle Armanyà side.

It is a new building, attached to the stagehouse, which substitutes another

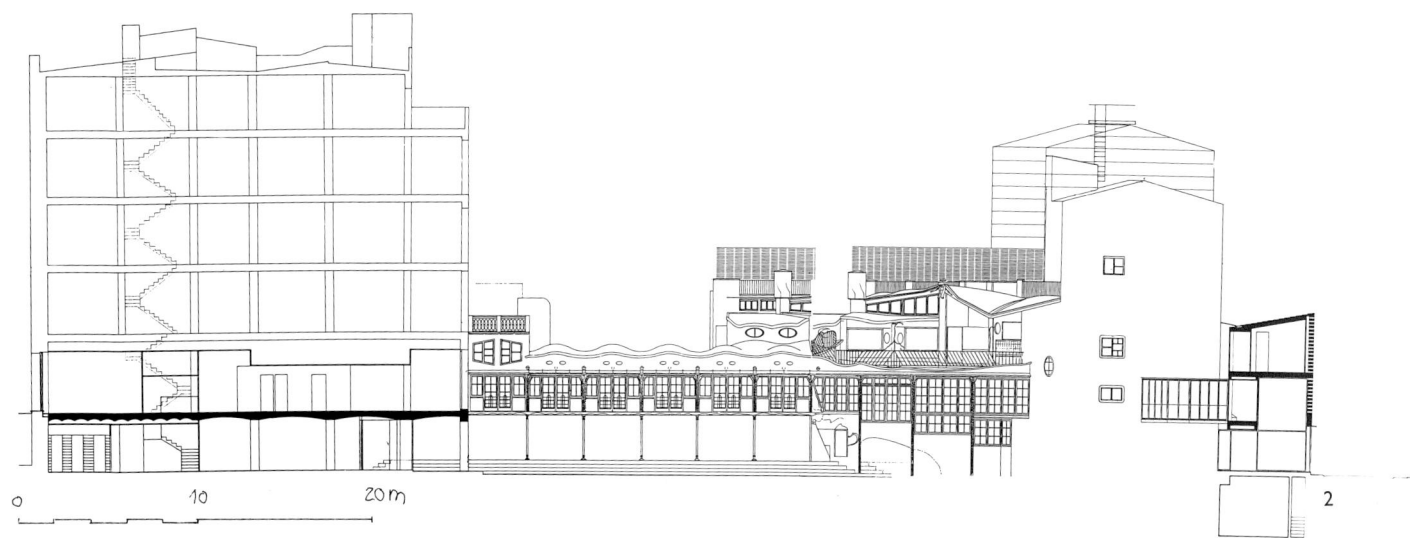

2 Longitudinal section through courtyard. Basic design

that existed before Jujol was brought in. It has been kept lower than the original, to fit into the scale on Calle Armanyà, a narrow secondary street, and also shallower, to increase the distance from Jujol's gallery.

The façade onto the courtyard was closed as a gallery, whose heights and divisions are similar to Jujol's; they are also similar to those of all the rear façades of the houses opening onto this courtyard. It is like defining the raw base that Jujol then manipulated, transformed and dematerialised, e.g., in the gallery from the Rambla Nova. In our case, its definition was just to display its material attributes.

B. ORTHODOX RECONSTRUCTION WORK
This criterion was applied to the remains of the gallery destroyed by bombs and then reconstructed with no reference to the original. There was sufficient data in the work (two out of six structural units were intact, as well as the main structure, parts of the ironwork, etc.) to remake the four damaged structural units with the same inverted domes as the originals. It seemed vital to do this reconstruction to recover the idea of the wave surging from the stalls stairway and breaking onto the vertical volume of the Rambla Nova building, its passage structured in six independent units from the courtyard. In doing so we used the same ingenious building system as the original, which was surprisingly more economical than a conventional system.

C. WORK MODIFYING JUJOL'S DESIGN
This was the most delicate part of the commission due to the lack of any original documentation, so that there was only the building itself, as it stood, to go on.

But, at the same time, this was also the most inspired, personal part: halfway between naïve spontaneity and the joyful invention of the world of theater, in which aquatic and religious references can become indissoluble. It was also the refurbishing part which did most damage to the original when the theater was turned into a cinema. This was where the lavatories were put in, part of the gallery closed, stairs and pillars hidden, etc.

It is hard to explain the work in just a few lines. The decisions taken were guided by the idea of masses of water advancing and retreating, just where the gallery ends and the theater hall begins; the boat sailing on these shifting seas (recalling Jujol's desire to turn the theater into a lifeboat); the attempt to reencounter the pleasingly domestic, modest scale of these marginal spaces; to underline the fundamental role of the carved brick pillar that articulates the passage from the gallery to the theatre hall, and so on.

The transformation into a cinema demolished balustrades, built walls to shut out the natural light, etc.

1 Access gallery
2 Access gallery, stagehouse and dressing rooms

The theater was cleared of all the additions, and extra wooden structures were used to change the rake in order to improve the stage visibility.

For safer egress, a new stair was added parallel to the existing one and treated as a younger version of it.

Besides this, there is a critical example of what we did: we tried to reconstruct the original balustrades from a photograph that captivated us.

The photograph (the only one we had then of the original hall) and our idea about the water-line being at the dress-circle level made us think that the balustrade was an expression of the water, a wave surging up on the verge of breaking.

The information gleaned from the photograph and this idea of leaping water was reflected in the first drawing and models. Two architects, Joan Vera and Claudia Thomet, then spent two months on the site, with chicken wire and mortar first, and then with burlap and plaster, helped by the plasterers and building workers on the site, until they achieved the result shown in the photograph, which we all liked. By all, I mean the architects, the plasterers, the builders, the works foreman, the works manager, etc. Even so, the result lacked the Jujol touch, as became increasingly clear. Finally, after several visits, still overwhelmed by doubts, we had it demolished. Everyone felt very sad about it. In fact, the works manager delayed the decision several days, until it began to seriously interfere with the building process.

3 Gallery at courtyard level. At the back, three V-shaped walls support the stairway to the stalls

Later, when the building was finished, some photographs of the original balustrade appeared, which cast some doubt on our interpretation.

It was lucky, then, that we demolished it in time. But, in all honesty, I think I preferred our interpretation to the reality shown in the latest photographs.

This anecdote is only intended to illustrate the difficulties and doubts we had in resolving the project in many cases where we only had clues, some more reliable than others, to the original theater: the closing of the stalls level from the courtyard; the location of the curtains; the artificial light; the definition of the light shaft behind the stalls; the necessary structural supports; the colors, etc.

1 The brick pillar articulating the passage from the gallery to the theater hall, on the second floor, supports a fan-shaped structure of iron girders

2 The same pillar on the lower floor, with the same load-bearing mission, is livened up with agitated waters and paintings by Jujol himself, with plant motifs and crowned "M's" (for Mary)

1

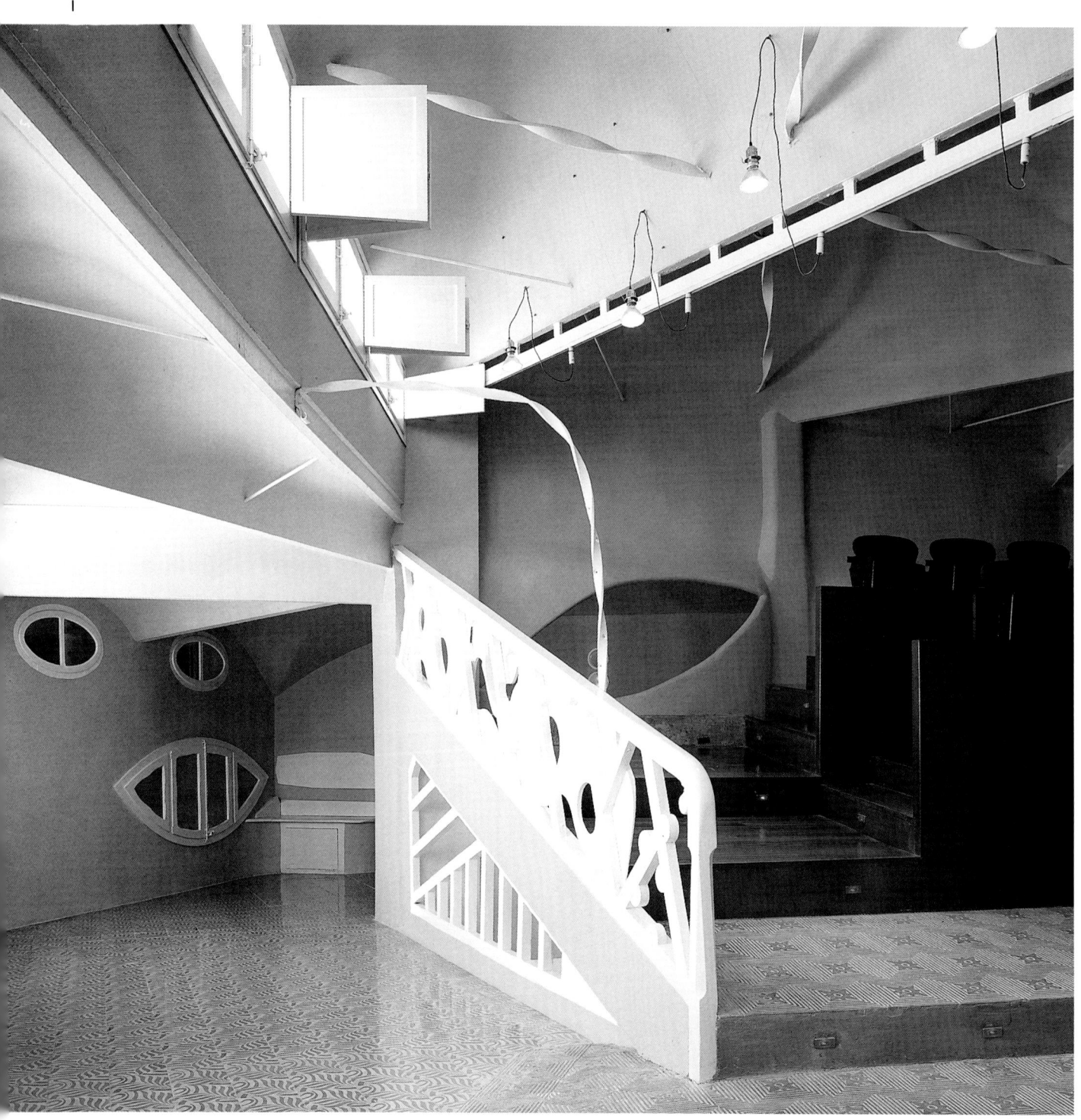

3 The same pillar on the stalls-level floor (underwater) with encrusted sea snails and fish

4 and 5 Stairway down to the courtyard, with waves and fish drawn on the steps

1 From here, the back of the upper circle, the amphitheater can be seen through eye-shaped openings. To the right, the public access gallery

2 The three levels of the theatre open up onto the courtyard shared with the rest of the block, using second-hand carved woodwork

DEVELOPER Tarragona City Council
COLLABORATING ARCHITECT Joan Vera
SURVEYOR Jaume Martí Almestoy
CONSTRUCTION COMPANY Fomento de Construcciones y Contratas, s.a.

1

2

Collblanc Primary School
Collblanc 136
Barcelona
1987-1996
In collaboration with Carlos Llinás Carmona, architect

The site was located at the end of a block whose planning regulations proposed the construction of two 11-storey towers. One of these was already built on the west edge of the site. The surrounding buildings were all relatively recent detached buildings seven or eight storeys high, laid out without any common nexus amongst themselves or with the street, either in terms of their geometrical shape or their volumetric delimitation.

The built-up environment in which the school was to be situated was therefore relatively low-grade. No shared guidelines could be found that might, however implicitly, bring the area together and influence the design of the school.

This lack of what we might call urban cohesion or urbanity made it hard to "get into" the environment, just as it is difficult to understand people lacking in urban courtesy, without being the same as them. Here that meant building big. But the best kind of school is not necessarily big and should not be high-rise. In fact, the first sketches of the preliminary design placed it parallel to the 11-storey building, at the other end of the site and shaped like a medicine capsule, but the result looked like a ridiculous miniature copy of the neighbors.

It was evident that the enormous 11-storey block on the west would be unavoidably present for people moving inside the school. Indeed it would be so pervasive that when the pupils became adults, they might well remember not so much the school building itself but, rather, the giant opposite.

Finally, having chosen the cylindrical shape, located on the highest point of the ground, like a tower looking out in all directions and none, the building seemed to have taken on an identity, affirmed in its geometry (in relation to the neighboring buildings through its size) and also seemed able to act as a point of reference in the urban environment, articulating the two streets, Calle Pisuerga and Calle Cardenal Reig.

The design was finished in 1987. Later it was revised in 1993-94 for economic reasons. The main change introduced in the design affected the central schoolyard, onto which the corridors open, which had been open-air and landscaped, but is now covered.

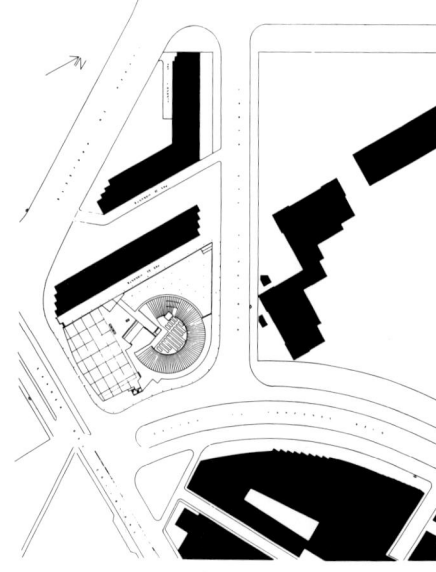

Area map
Access seen from inside

1 Façade onto Calle Pisuerga and Calle Cardenal Reig
2 Floor plan of first design
3 to 6 Floor plans
7 Section of first design
8 Section
9 Building access
10 West elevation
11 East elevation

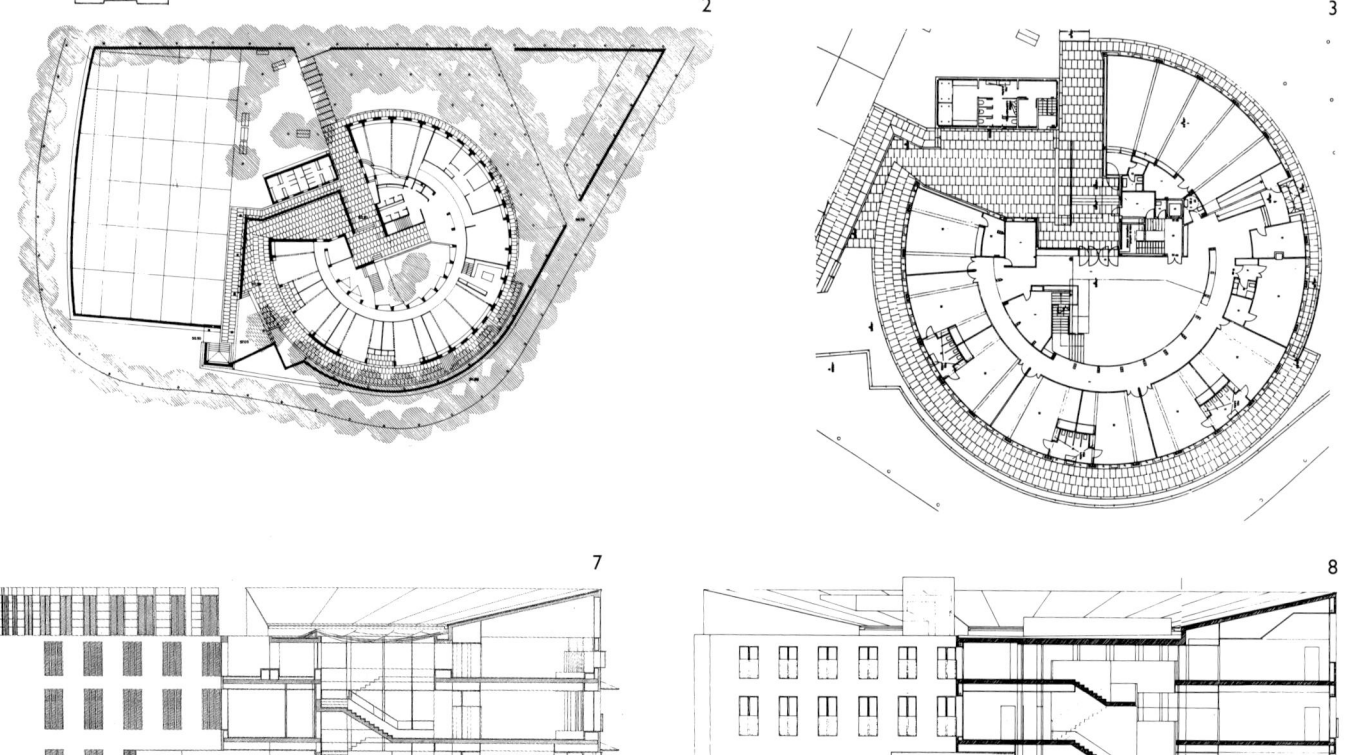

9

4

5

6

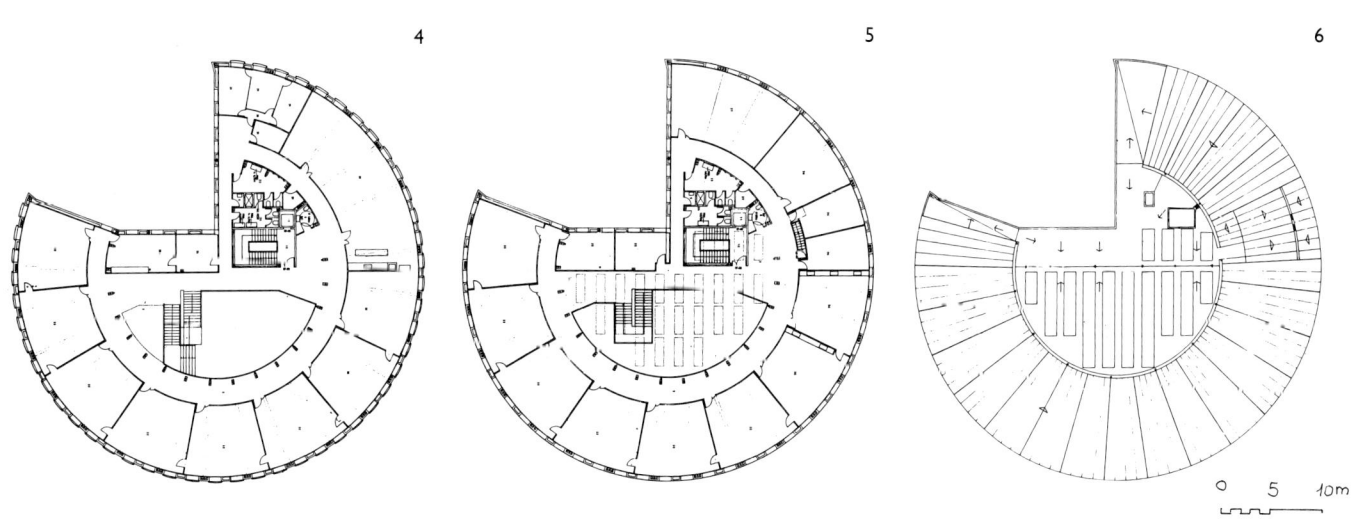

10

11

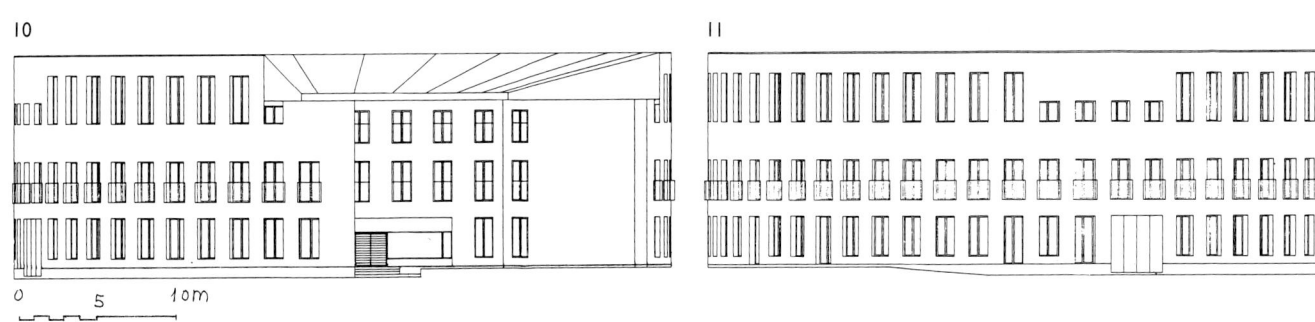

1 Courtyard central core. Detail
2 View from upper corridor to stairs
3 View from courtyard stairs

DEVELOPER Barcelona City Council
SURVEYOR Jaume Casas
CONSTRUCTION COMPANY Movilma, Teyco

Apartment Building on Calle Carme
Carme 55-57 and Roig 28-36
Barcelona
1992-1995

Although the municipal planning regulations permitted total occupation of the site (and this could almost have been considered obligatory), it was hard to propose a continuous building, 15 or 16 m. high, giving onto a street only 4 m. wide, and this not so much because of the quality of the resulting buildings, but more because it meant renouncing the possibility of doing something about the starkness of the Calle Roig.

Increasing its quality as a street, an instrument of communication, was possible given the front, which was almost 50 m. long.

The first step, then, was to open it up in a funnel shape towards the Calle Carme, to take advantage of the street's hustle and bustle. This change of alignment affected the ground floor (average height 5.5 m.), and created visual communication between Calle Carme and Calle Hospital via the Calle Roig.

Three almost independent housing blocks were laid out on this newly aligned site, more or less running along the new line.

The one on the Carme/Roig corner recovered the original opening; the one located further down Calle Roig supported and reinforced the new alignment; and the third, withdrawn and hardly visible from the street, helped to obtain the minimum number of housing units that the developer needed to build in order to make the project feasible.

Insisting on the desire to relate houses and street properly, the living rooms were put on the corners, seeking views along Calle Roig.

Ground floor occupation as per regulations

Proposed ground floor occupation

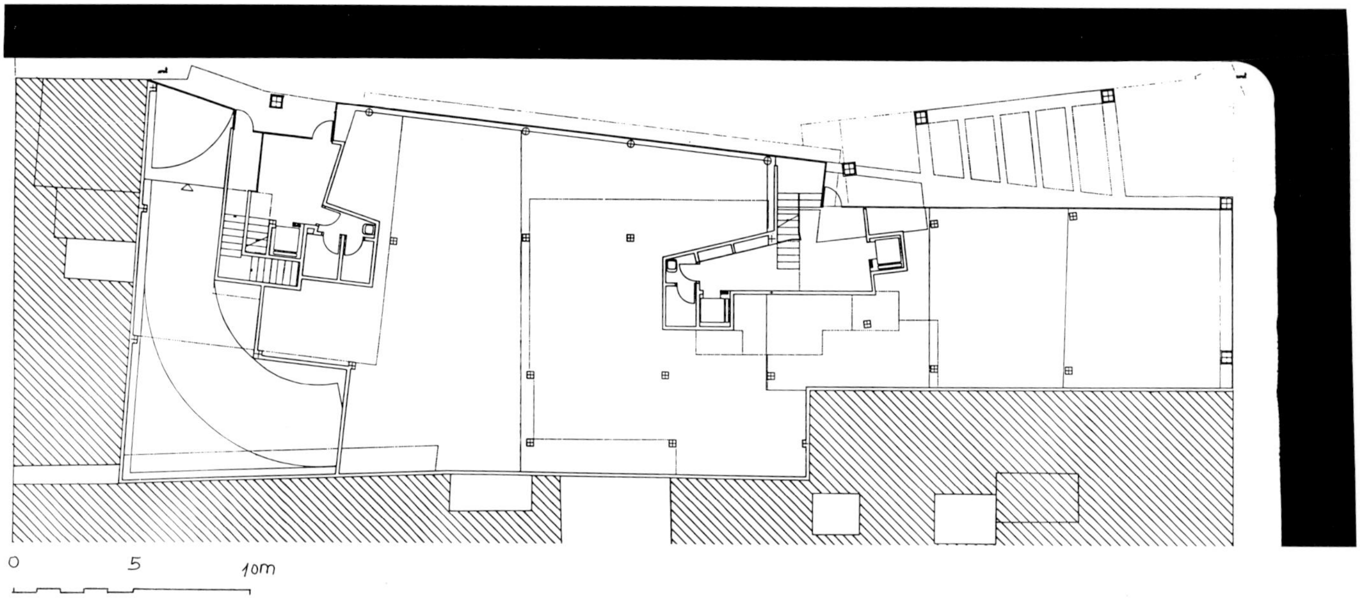

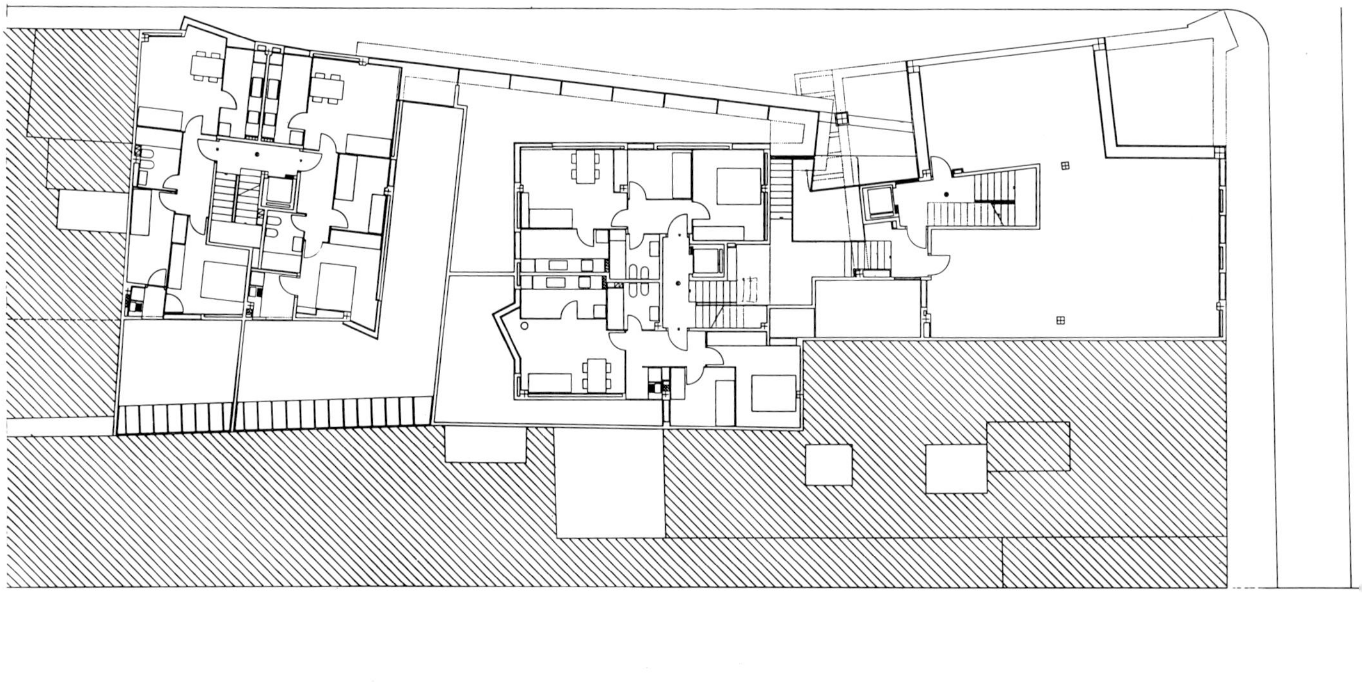

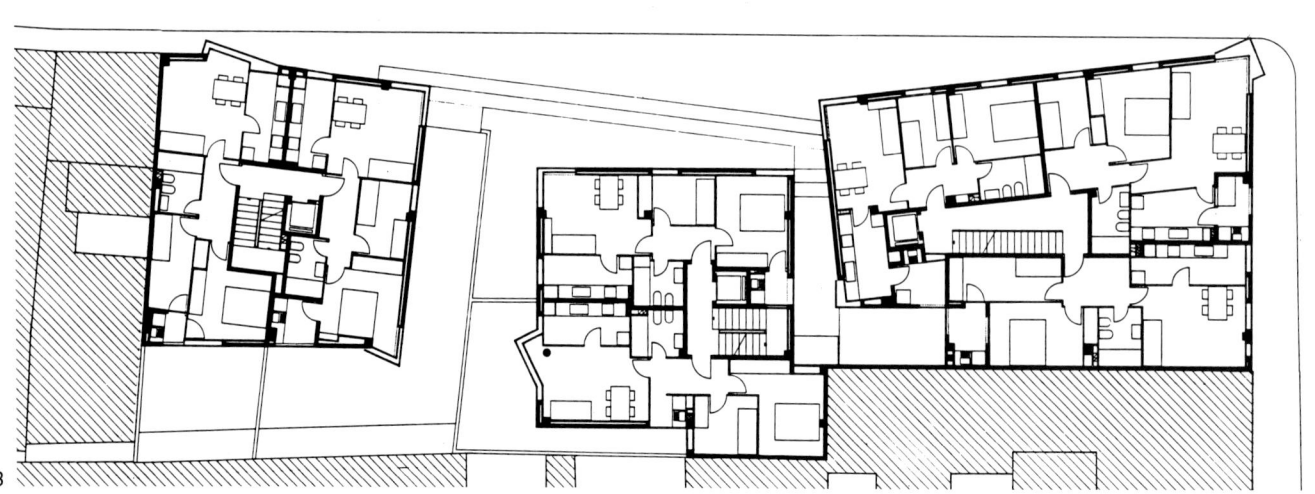

1 Ground floor plan
2 First floor plan
3 Standard floor plan
4 Calle Carme façade
5 Aerial perspective
6 Elevations to Calle Carme and Calle Roig

4

5

6

0 5m

1 Perspective from Calle Carme
2 Carme-Roig street corner
3 Beginning of Calle Roig
4 Shared entrance to first two buildings

3

4

1 Buildings from Calle Roig looking towards Calle Carme
2 Shared access to first two buildings

DEVELOPER PROCIVESA
SURVEYOR Jaume Martí Almestoy
CONSTRUCTION COMPANY Contratas y Obras, s.a.

Computer Department Building
Module B2. Campus Nord
Universidad Politécnica de Barcelona
1993-1995

The building was to be located on the edge of the Universidad Politécnica de Barcelona, whose regular layout is governed by the campus planning statutes.

From the outset, the density of buildings on the campus made it desirable to lighten the volume and the appearance of the Computer Department building, which had to be of red brick, according to the campus planning statutes.

Looking at the use specifications, it became clear that there was no need to occupy all the available surface area at ground level, since underground occupation was suitable for many requirements: much of the building was to be used for the Computer Department's Calculation Center.

Two layers were taken out of the original parallelepiped: one in relation to the square to the west, in order to make an access terrace linked to the square, and the other related to the street to the south, to distance the building from its neighbors.

The next task consisted of adding white metal galleries to the volumes resulting from this operation, in order to soften the monotony of the red brick.

Cutting up and eliminating the regular prism or mould that the planning statutes established, which extended to the skyline, allowed the building to take on an individual character, separating it from the typical administration block and thus revealing its separate identity.

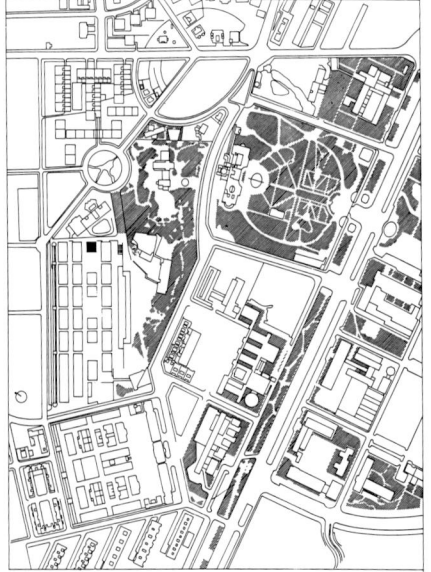

Area map
South façade

1 Axonometric projection of the building and surrounding area in the campus plan
2 to 7 Floor plans
8 West façade
9 and 10 Sections through access courtyard
Preceding pages: main stairwell

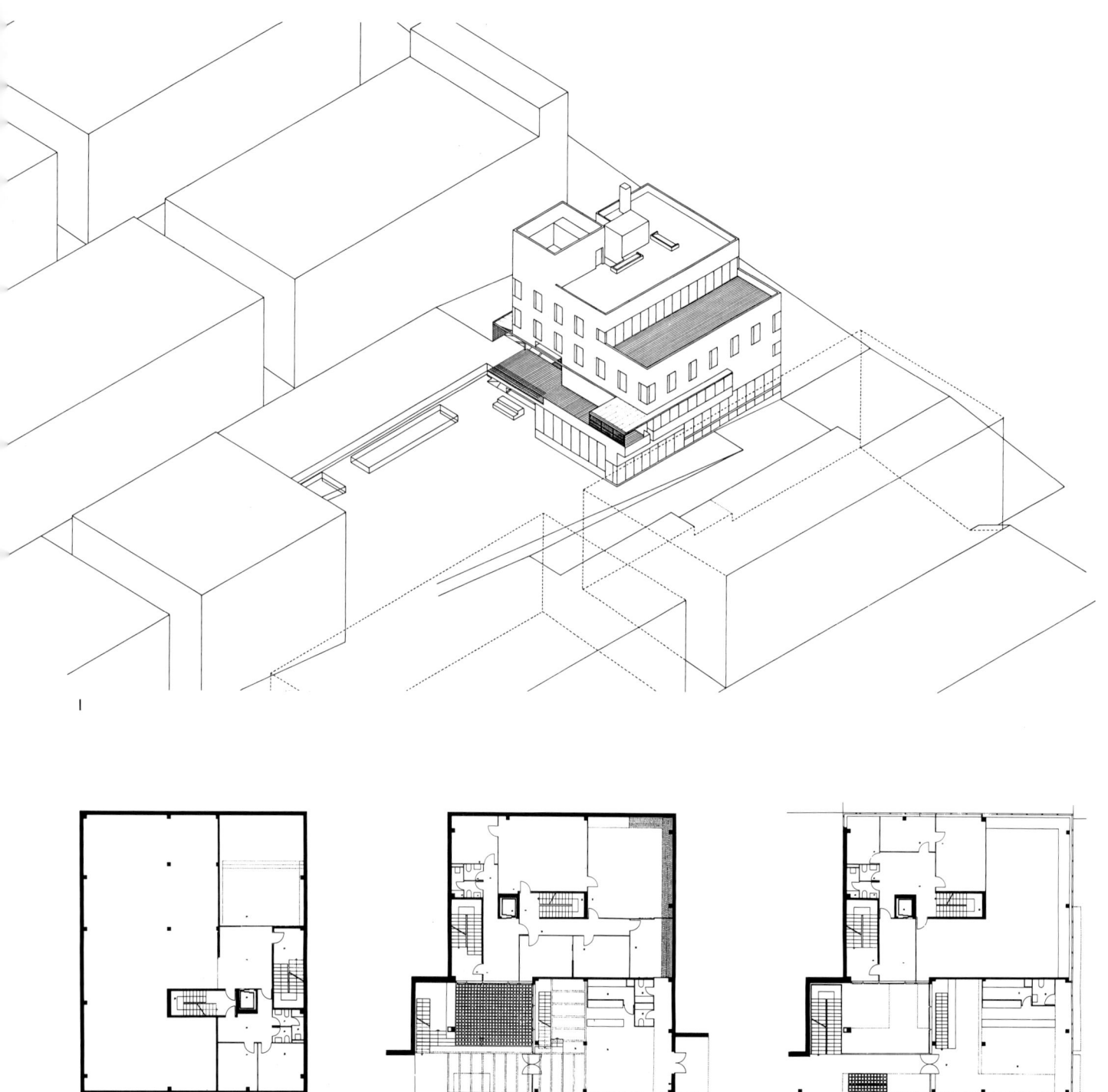

8

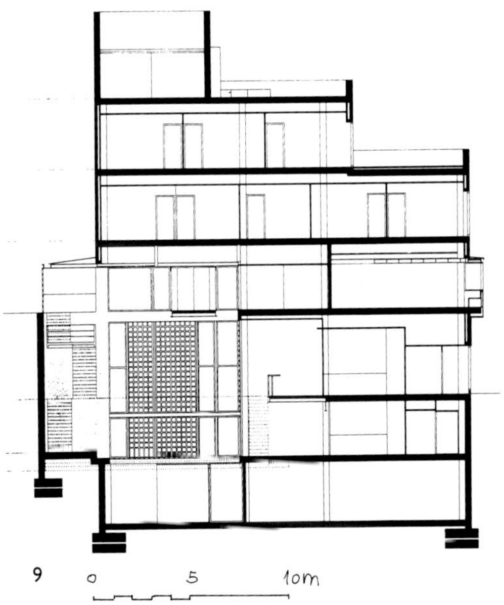

9 0 5 10m
10

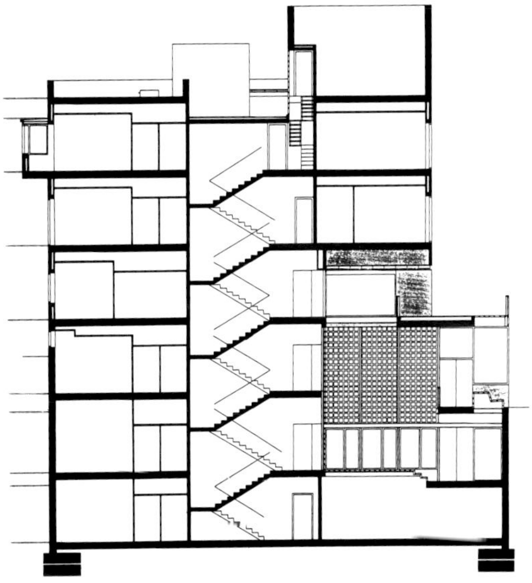

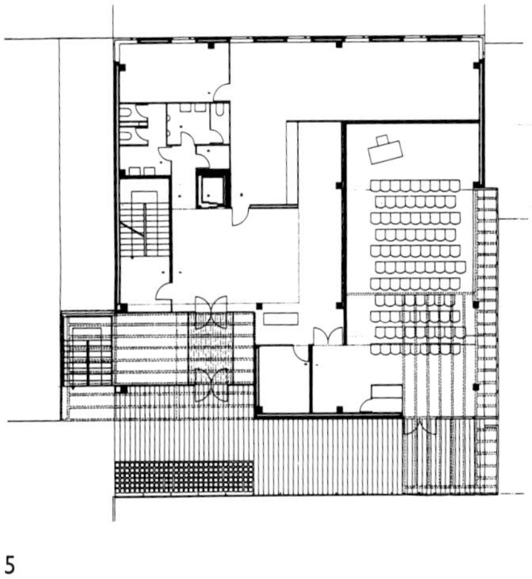

5 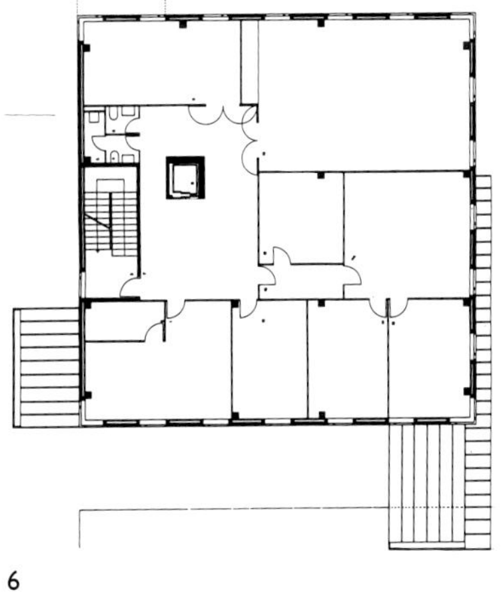 6 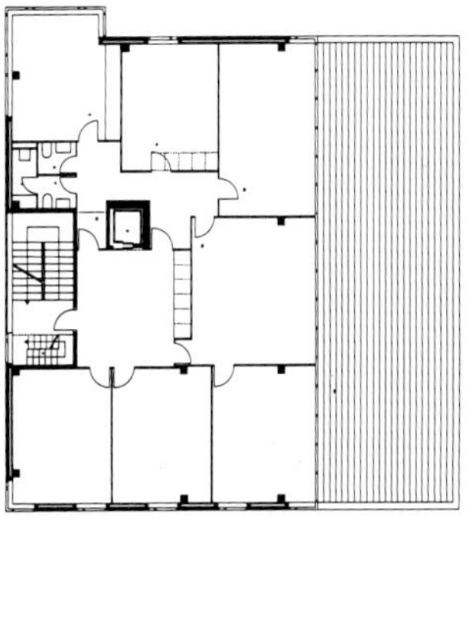 7

123

1 Main entrance level

2 Access courtyard from floor −2

1 Access staircase to service area
2 Conference room

1

1 Access courtyard
2 Second floor terrace

2

DEVELOPER Universidad Politécnica de Barcelona
SURVEYOR Jaume Martí Almestoy
CONSTRUCTION COMPANIES Construcciones San José, s.a. and Dragados y Construcciones, s.a.

Law School Lecture Rooms and Bar
Facultad de Derecho, Universidad de Barcelona
Pedralbes, Barcelona
1993-1996

The lecture room and bar building was to be constructed on a key site, on the slope between the Law School, one of the most exceptional buildings on campus and, above it, what used to be the Lérida Students' Residence, or Colegio Mayor Ilerdense, now used for the Law School departments.

The strip of ground stood between two very different types of building: the vertical, five-storey block of the former Students' Residence and the rigorously horizontal formation of the Law School. Besides, it also formed part of the large area of lawns and trees surrounding the Law School, stretching up to the former Students' Residence, an exceptional amount of open space given the density of built land on campus.

Immediately, a clear idea of the section came to mind, embedding the building into the earth, as if it were behind a trench, to keep as much of the lawns and trees and alter the topography of the site as little as possible. The idea of a sloping copper roof also came at once. The way copper changes over time makes it seem to share in nature's tendency to change, and the slope would establish a parallelism with the sloping ground.

During the design stage, the long lecture room and bar building (85 m.) adapted itself like a scarf to the very high block of the former Students' Residence.

The building was divided into three parts. One of these was established to enable pedestrians to get around the lecture rooms, the teaching areas and the former Students' Residence. These three parts were laid out on a line, aligned either with the street, the Law School or the Students' Residence.

The building was intentionally constituted more around the idea of a country house, subject (perhaps somewhat artificially) to the topographical constraints of the site, than to an urban building, although it forms part of the city.

The materials chosen and the laws regulating their use determined the final look of the building.

Area map
South façade

1 Section

2 to 6 Plans

7 Passageway between bar and lecture rooms, and access stairs to bar terrace

8 Aerial view from the former Students' Residence, the Colegio Mayor Ilerdense

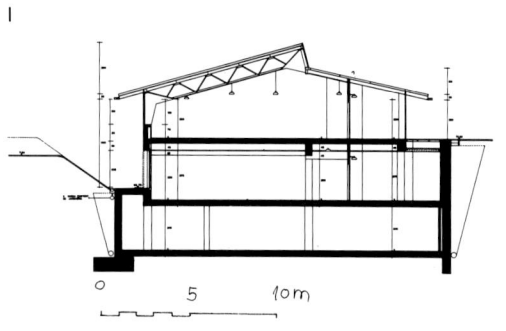

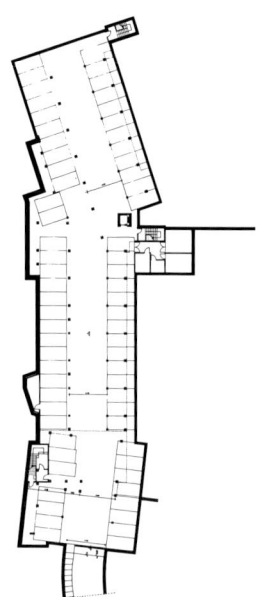

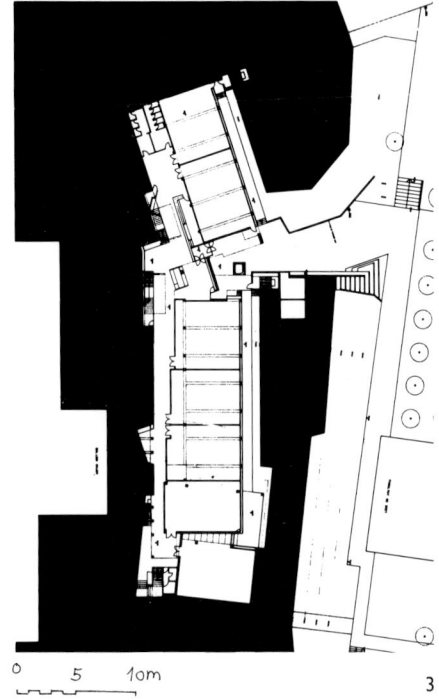

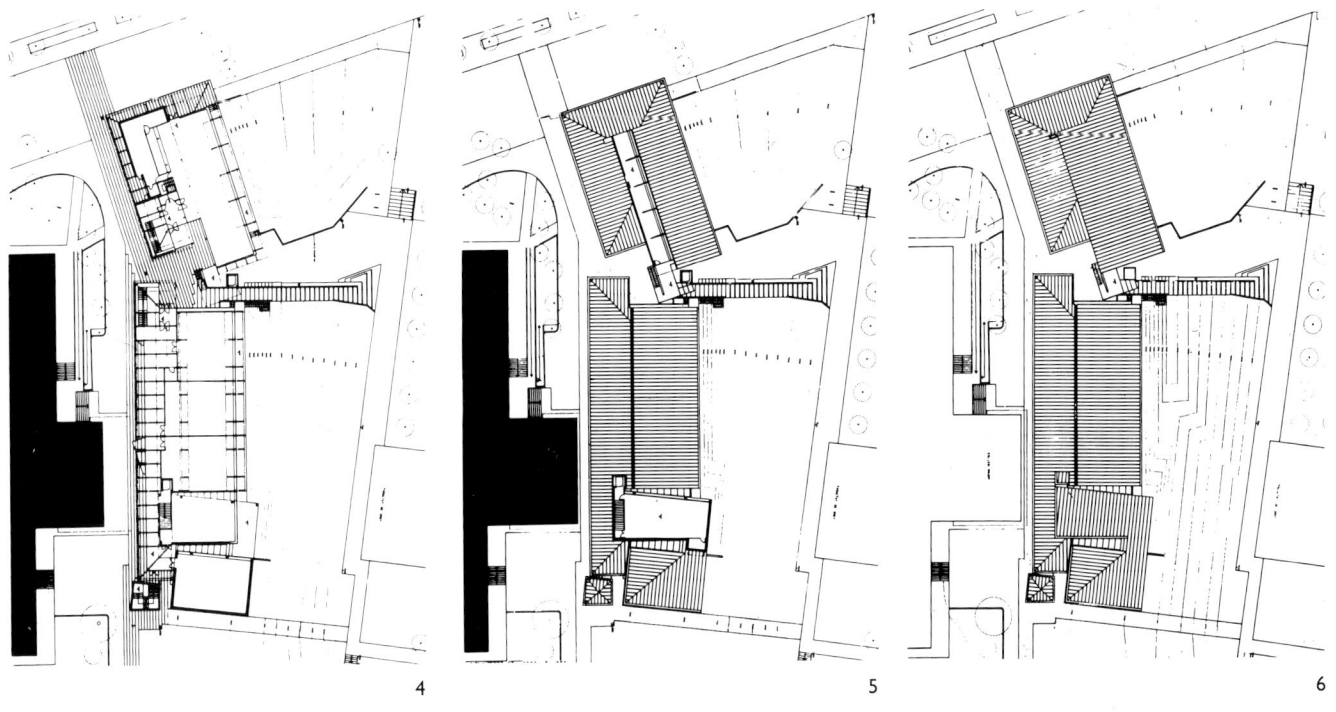

4
5
6
8

1 Western tip of south façade
2 Western tip of building, as seen from the former Students' Residence

1 Western tip of north façade, looking to the former Students' Residence
2 Stairs to hall on lower floor

3 Bar interior

Interior of lecture room

DEVELOPER Universidad de Barcelona
SURVEYORS Jaume Martí Almestoy and Joan Ardévol
CONSTRUCTION COMPANIES OCP, Dragados y Construcciones, s.a. and Rubau, s.a.

Secondary School
Avenida Sant Jordi 62
Torredembarra, Tarragona
1993-1996

Compared to most of the commissions received to date, this one was superbly situated on a small hill on the edge of Torredembarra and had splendid views in all directions: out over the sea and over the softly rolling Tarragona landscape.

The site's specifications were also very favorable: more than enough room to meet the building program; a slight seaward slope; and communication with the town only on the west edge. The other edges bordered on natural landscape.

The only built-up edge, on the west, was made up of an extensive area of isolated, detached houses leading up to the town center.

The design, a regular, square-shaped building with a big central courtyard, both met the program and gave rise to a correct relationship between access passageways and working space.

During the design stage, it was decided to close part of the indeterminate outside space in a courtyard, so that the building somehow appropriated some of the qualities of the open air in Tarragona: the limpid light, the temperature, the sunshine...

Controlling this air, propitiating the formation of a kind of microclimate, covering the courtyard and protecting it from direct sunlight, was one of the design's fundamental aims. In opposition to the disaggregated architecture of the group of detached houses on the way from the town to the school, this had a compact volume that would identify and affirm it as a public building which purposely exhibited its cubic origins, its size and its centrality.

The resulting parallelepiped (39 x 39 x 10 m.) underwent two final changes before construction:

1. A single storey was segregated to the west, for the administration offices, set towards the entrance like a forward outpost of the building to receive people coming from the town.

2. The horizontal line defining the upper limit of the building was artificially warped in order to establish a dialogue or exchange with the enormous blue plane of the sky, which is a fundamental part of the landscape in Tarragona.

Area map
Courtyard

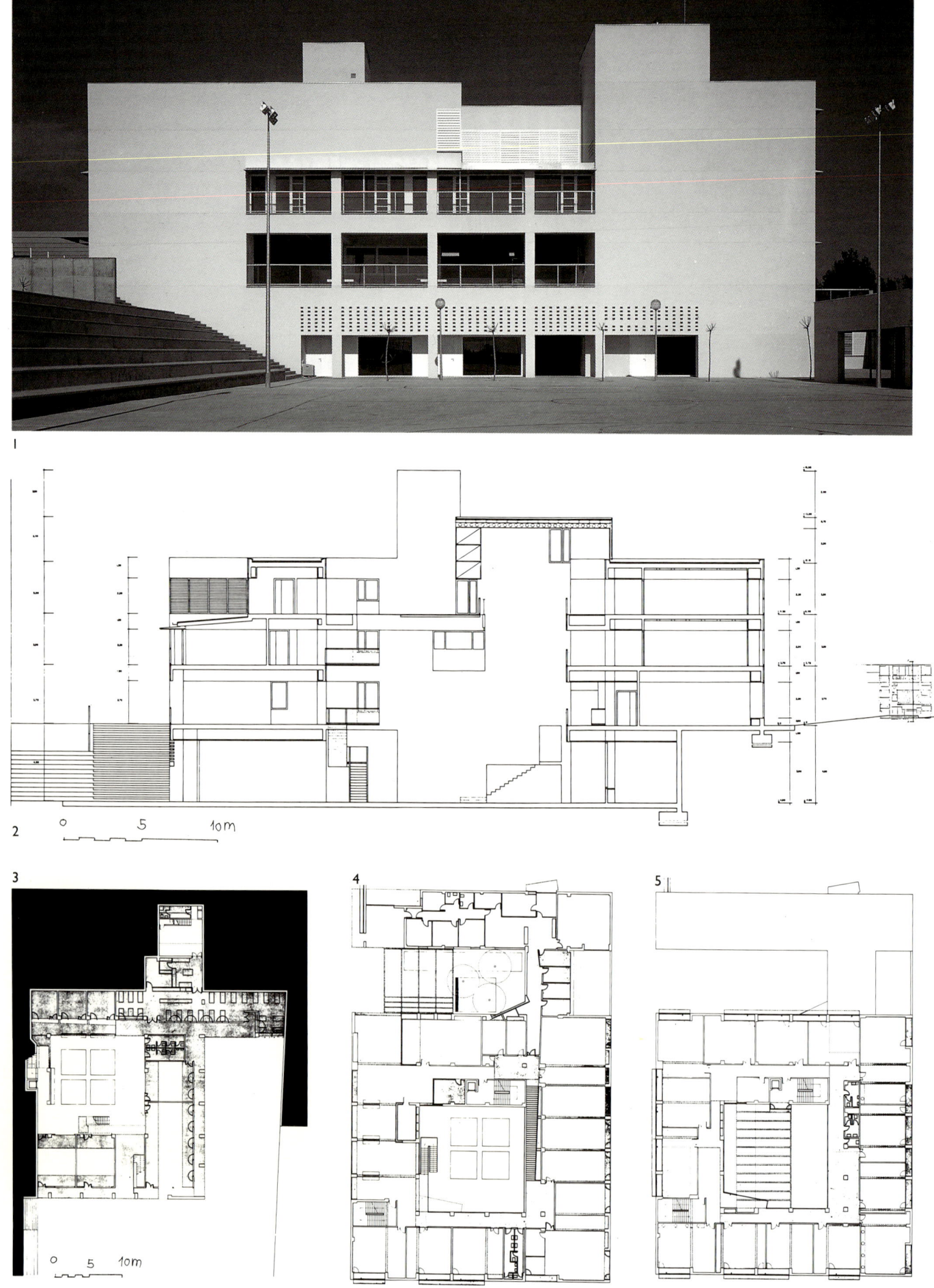

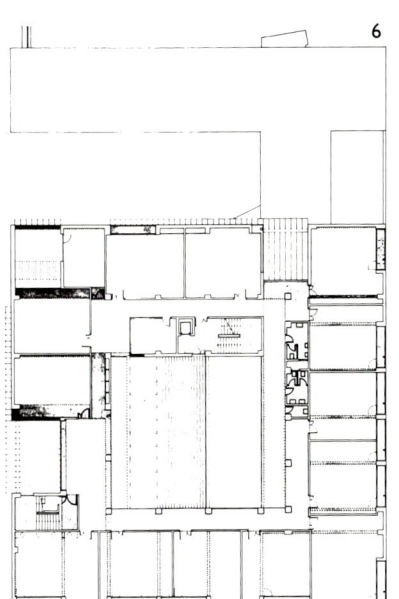
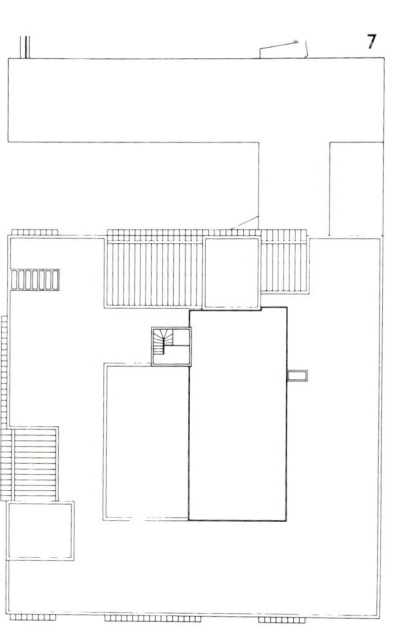
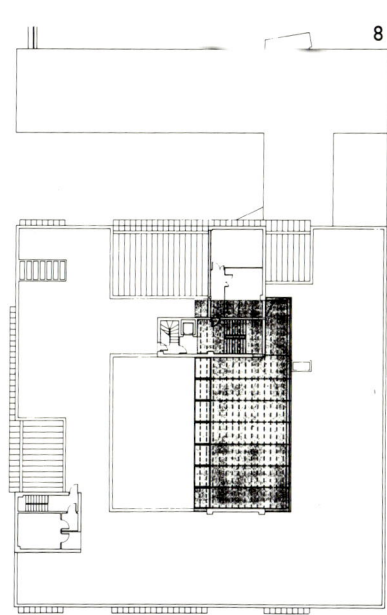

1 South façade
2 Section
3 to 8 Floor plans
9 Inner courtyard

1 and 2 Courtyard
3 Pergola connecting the low single-storey administration building with the teaching building

1 and 6 North elevation and façade
2 South elevation
3 and 5 East elevation and façade
4 West elevation

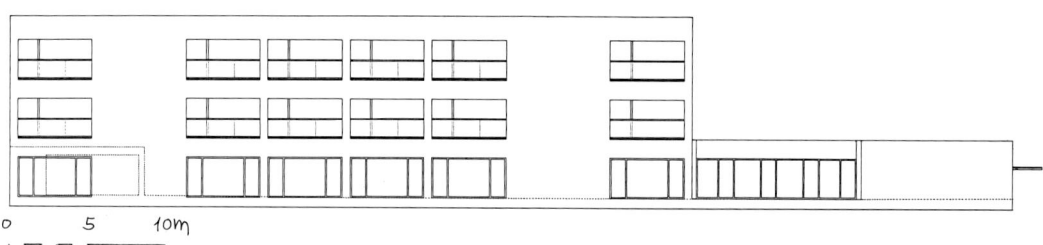

1

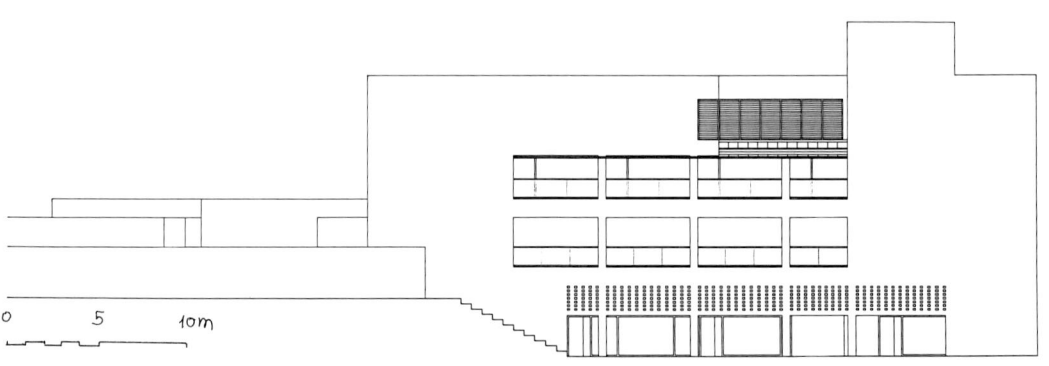

2

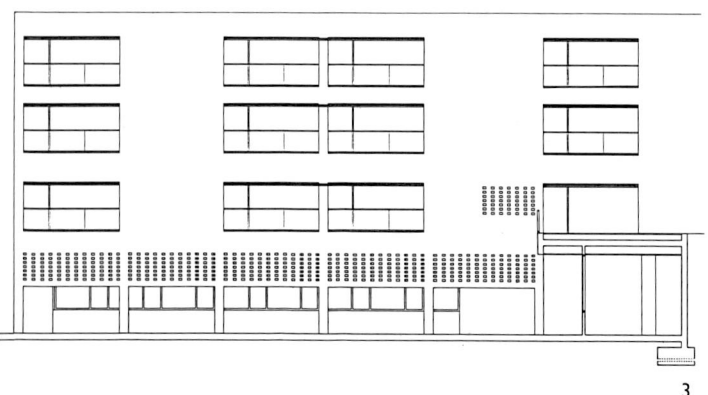

3

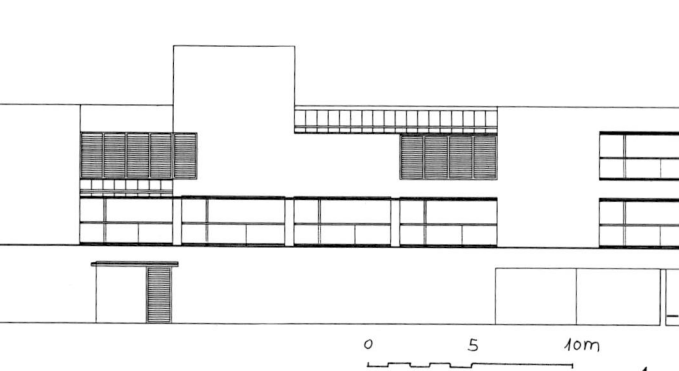

4

5

6

Access to the building on west façade

1 and 2 Courtyard from the second floor

2

DEVELOPER Teaching Department, Catalonian Regional Government
STRUCTURES Robert Brufau
SURVEYOR Jaume Martí Almestoy
CONSTRUCTION COMPANY Vicsan, s.a.

Apartment Buildings and Shops
Conegliano, Italy
1995

The commission required building four apartment buildings – three on a square plan and one as a block – in the context of a general plan drawn up by Boris Prodecca on the site of the old Zanussi factory in Conegliano. The search for urbanity and, in a sense, anonymity, lies at the heart of the design. Here, this attitude was adopted, perhaps even more strongly than in other commissions, in order to build the blocks as part of the city. The design is the outcome of instruments deriving purely from professional experience.

1

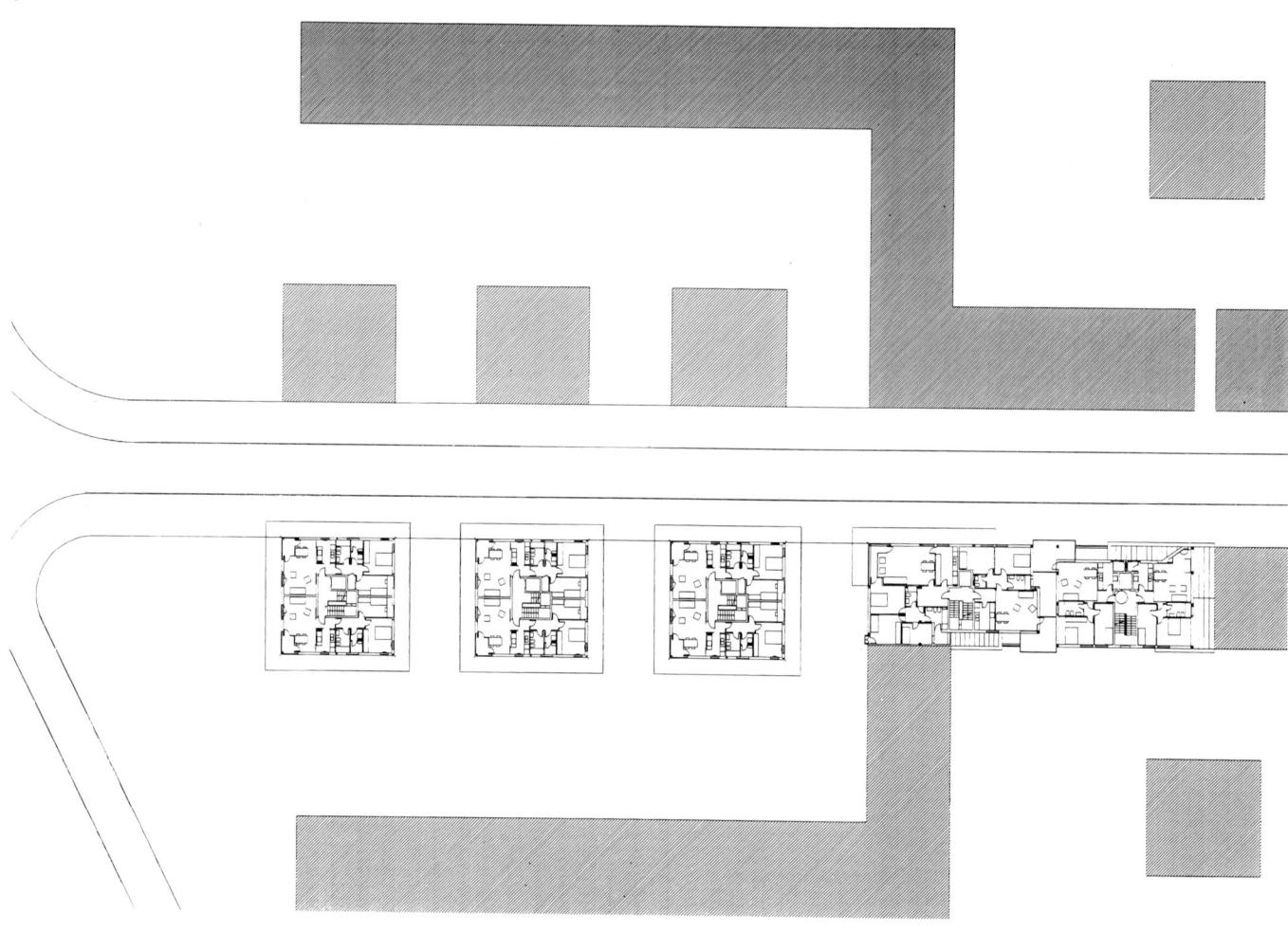

1 General plan
2 and 3 Different perspectives of the three separate buildings from the street

Works and Projects

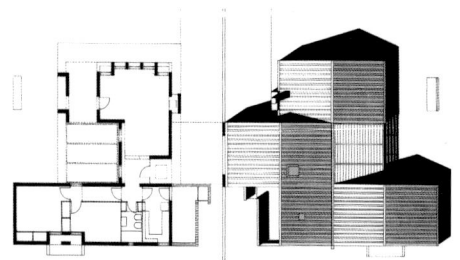

Detached House in Cala'n Bosch
Urbanización Cala'n Bosch, plot 9.A
Ciutadella. Menorca
With Xavier Surinyach López
1969-1970

El Carmelo Housing Block
Pere Costa 25. Barcelona
1971-1972

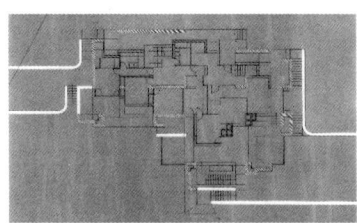

Detached House in Monistrol de Calders
Camino de Sant Pere Mártir s/n
Monistrol de Calders. Barcelona
1970-1973

Bibliography: 74

Housing Block (with 23 apartments) between party walls, in Ferreríes
Carretera de Maó a Ciutadella, Km 28
Ferreríes. Menorca
1971-1974

Bibliography: 9, 73, 167

Housing Block between party walls in Berga
Rasa del Canyet s/n
Berga. Barcelona
1973-1977

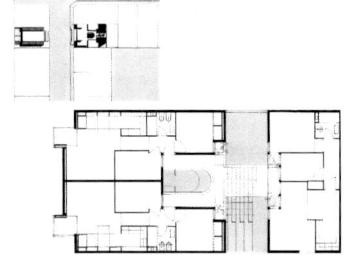

Apartment Block between party walls in Rosas
Doctor Fleming s/n
Rosas. Gerona
1972-1974

Bibliography: 72

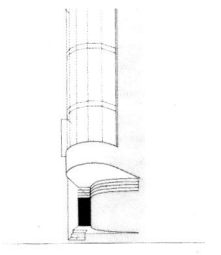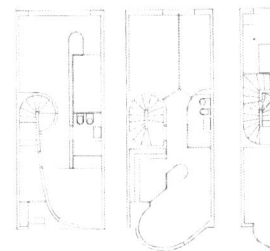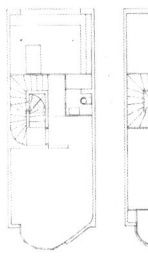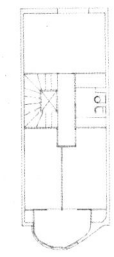

Apartment Block between party walls in Torredembarra
Barrio marítimo, Torredembarra
Tarragona
Not executed
1976

Bibliography: 77, 166

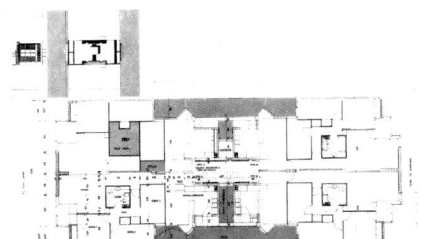

Housing Block (with 24 apartments)
Sant Jaume s/n
Vilafranca del Penedés. Barcelona
1975-1977

Bibliography: 75, 216

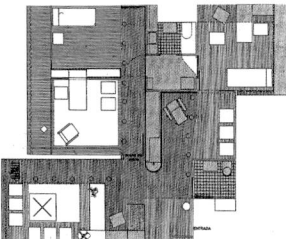

Remodelling Work for a Doctor's Surgery
Muntaner 505. Barcelona
1977-1978

Bibliography: 80

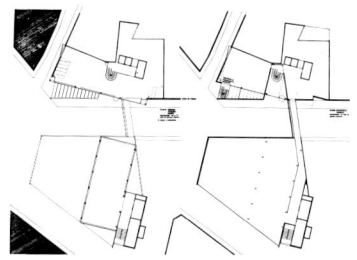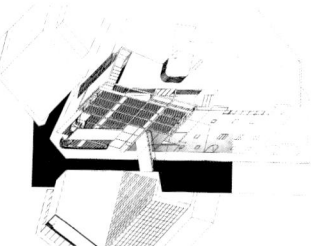

Extension to the Barcelona Professional College of Architects
Plaça Nova 5. Barcelona
COAC de Barcelona
Draft competition, not executed
1977

Bibliography: 78, 97, 98, 129

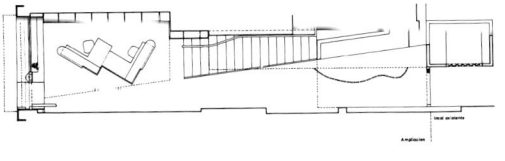

Remodelling Work for a Surgical Aids Shop
Enric Granados 131. Barcelona
1977

Bibliography: 29, 45, 79, 169, 178

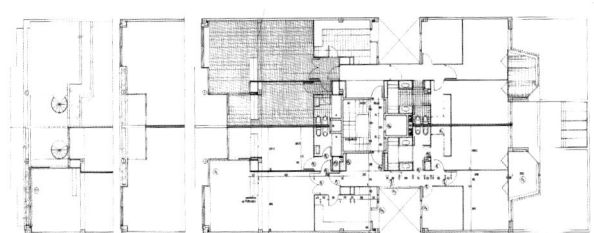

Housing Block (with 18 apartments) between party walls, in Vilafranca del Penedés
Misser Rufet 5
Vilafranca del Penedés. Barcelona
1978-1980

Bibliography: 44, 81, 124, 133, 160, 165, 168

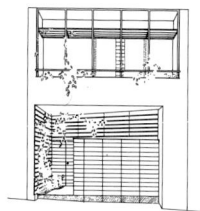 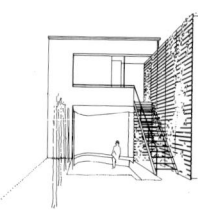

Detached House in Canet de Mar
Misericordia 16
Canet de Mar. Barcelona
1979-1980

Conservation - Restoration of the Monastery of Santa María de Ripoll
Ministry of Culture
Not executed
1980

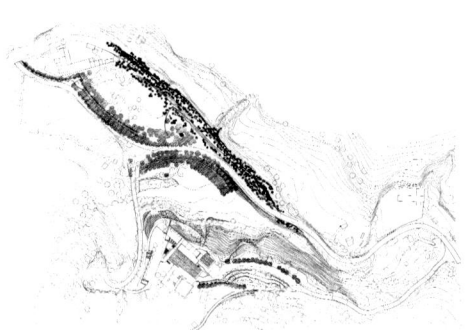 

Fitting out of the *La Salut* Public Area in Sant Feliú de Llobregat
Finca *La Salut*
Sant Feliú de Llobregat. Barcelona
Barcelona Metropolitan Corporation
1981-1986
Surveyor: Jaume Martí Almestoy
Structures: Robert Brufau
Construction: Lorenzo Parreu, s.a.

Bibliography: 30, 86, 93

Detached House in Begur
Urbanización Más Prats, plot 61
Carretera de Begur a Sa Tuna, Km 0.8
Begur. Gerona
1978-1980
Surveyor: Jaume Martí Almestoy
Structures: Robert Brufau
Construction: Narcís Fuster, s.a.

Bibliography: 1, 7, 28, 48, 50, 59, 61, 71, 82, 91, 114, 139, 170, 177, 187, 212

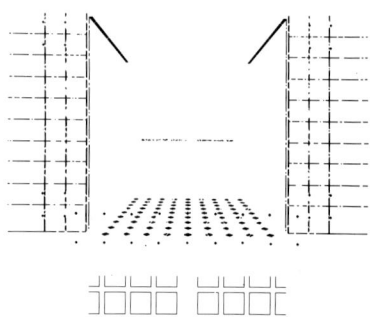 

Family Tomb at El Masnou Cemetery
El Masnou. Barcelona
1980

Bibliography: 27, 42, 43, 55, 83, 89, 101, 189, 211

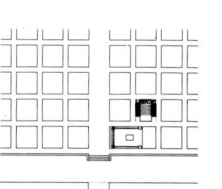 

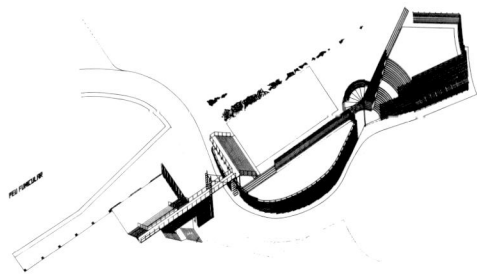

Distribution of the Vallvidrera Funicular Station
Avenida Vallvidrera - Carroz
First design, not executed
1982
A second design was executed in 1985
– see page 160

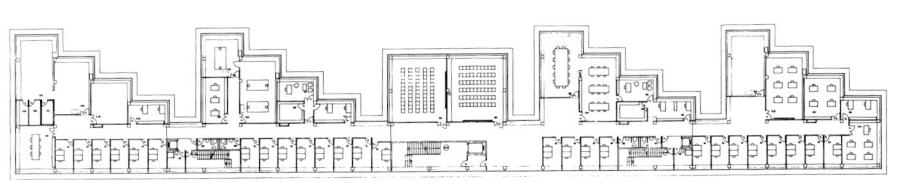

Geological Science School
Universidad Central de Barcelona
Martí Franqués 1-11. Barcelona
With José A. Martínez Lapeña, Elías Torres Tur and Miguel Usandizaga
Design: 1983
Execution: UCB Technical Unit

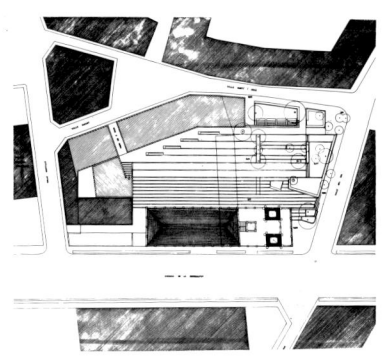 

Refurbishment and Extension to the Pallejà Town Hall and Block Distribution
Plaza del Ayuntamiento
Pallejà. Barcelona
Barcelona Metropolitan Corporation
Not executed
1983

Bibliography: 87

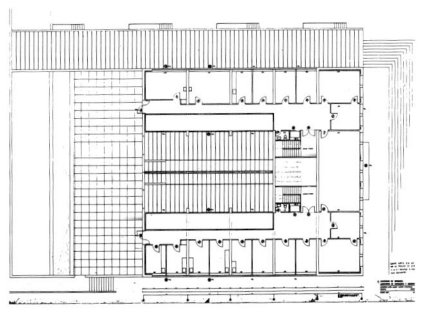

Microscopy and Spectroscopy Laboratory Buildings
Universidad Central de Barcelona
Martí Franqués 1-11. Barcelona
With José Antonio Martínez Lapeña, Elías Torres Tur and Miguel Usandizaga
Design: 1983
Execution: UCB Technical Unit

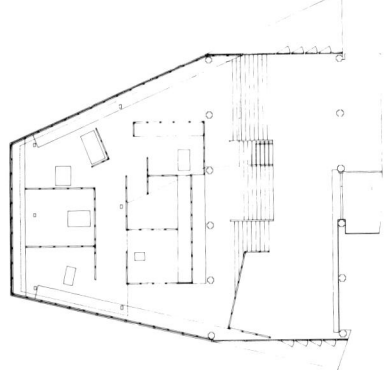 

"Montjuïc Olimpic" Exhibition Assembly
COAC de Barcelona
Plaça Nova 5. Barcelona
Barcelona City Council Office for the Olympics
1984

Primary Care Hospital in Ripollet
Parc Massot. Ripollet. Barcelona
INSALUD. Catalonian Regional Government
1982-1985
Surveyor: Jaume Martí Almestoy
Structures: Robert Brufau
Construction: Dragados y Construcciones, s.a.
Surface areas:
- Site: 19,374 m²
- Building: 2,610 m²
- Carpark: 2,854 m²
Bibliography: 4, 8, 25, 38, 46, 51, 58, 60, 62, 63, 67, 68, 85, 90, 104, 112, 114, 135, 137, 153, 174, 190, 199, 217

Distribution of the Vallvidrera Funicular Station (Second Design)
Avenida Vallvidrera - Carroz `
Barcelona
1984-1985
Surveyor: Jaume Martí Almestoy
Structures: Robert Brufau
Construction: Construcciones Cornadó, s.a.

Bibliography: 3, 26, 57, 70, 84, 103, 120, 130, 156, 188, 210

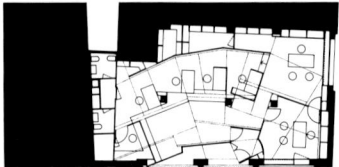

Refurbishment of a Bank's Branch Office in Gracia
Plaza Rovira i Trias. Barcelona
Not executed
1985

Bibliography: 23, 191, 197

Vilaseca Municipal Library
Vilaseca Town Council
Rambla de Catalunya s/n. Vilaseca
Tarragona
1985-1986
Surveyor: Jaume Martí Almestoy
Structures: Robert Brufau
Construction: Servicios y Obras, s.a.
Site surface area: 2,119 m²
Built surface area: 875 m²

Bibliography: 11, 15, 24, 155, 192

Restoration of the Tarragona Civilian Government Building
Plaza Imperial Tarraco. Tarragona
Ministry of the Interior
1985-1987
Architects: Alejandro de la Sota and Josep Llinás Carmona
Surveyors: Jaume Martí Almestoy and J. Ricomà
Fittings and equipment: F. Labastida
Construction: Fomento de Obras y Construcciones, s.a.

Bibliography: 12, 31, 125, 151, 154, 179, 193

Collblanc Primary School
Collblanc 136. Barcelona
Barcelona City Council
First design, not executed
1987
A second design was executed in 1996 – see page 166

Office and Apartment Building in Vilafranca del Penedés
Av. Tarragona 35
Vilafranca del Penedés. Barcelona
1988-1990
Surveyor: Jaume Martí Almestoy
Structures: Robert Brufau
Construction: Josep Salat, s.a.

Bibliography: 14

Distribution of the Montserrat Abbey Complex
Monistrol
Catalonian Regional Government, Culture Department
Competition, not executed
1987

Detached House in Sant Feliú de Llobregat
Vidal i Ribas 34
Sant Feliú de Llobregat. Barcelona
1986-1988
Surveyor: Jaume Martí Almestoy
Structures: Robert Brufau
Construction: P. Tomás, s.a.

Bibliography: 2, 22, 54, 76, 100, 117, 126, 157, 186

Extension to the Barcelona History Museum in the Marés Museum Courtyard
Plaça Sant Iu 5-6. Barcelona
Barcelona City Council
Draft design, not executed
1988

Bibliography: 21, 194, 198

Spanish Embassy in Paris
Av. Marceau 22-Georges V 13-15
Paris
1989-1992
Architect: Alejandro de la Sota
Overseers: Alejandro de la Sota and Josep Llinás Carmona
Consultants: Sereland, s.a.
Construction: Dragados y Construcciones, s.a.
Total useful surface area: 5,130 m²

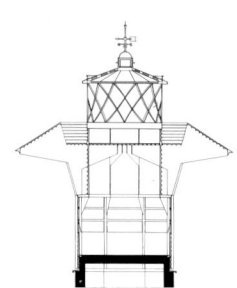

Torredembarra Lighthouse
Torredembarra. Tarragona
Ministry of Public Works and Town Planning
Not executed
1988

Bibliography: 18, 94

Refurbishment of the Barcelona Archaeological Museum
Passeig Santa Madrona 39-41. Barcelona
Barcelona Provincial Council
1984-1989
Surveyor: Jaume Martí Almestoy
Structures: Robert Brufau
Fittings and equipment: O.I.T.
Construction: Fomento de Obras y Construcciones, s.a.
Built surface area: 1,960 m²

Bibliography: 6, 16, 33, 34, 35, 53, 64, 66, 88, 89, 95, 99, 108, 109, 113, 116, 118, 131, 132, 134, 135, 141, 158, 175, 180, 200, 213

Engineering School Library, Lecture Rooms and Departments
Modules 15 and 16, Campus Nord
Universidad Politécnica de Barcelona
Barcelona
1987-1989
Surveyor: Jaume Martí Almestoy
Structures: Robert Brufau
Fittings and equipment: O.I.T.
Construction: Deco, s.a.
Built surface areas: 1,153 m² (Library); 2,870 m² (Departments)

Bibliography: 5, 20, 37, 39, 56, 65, 69, 96, 102, 107, 115, 120, 127, 128, 144, 159, 196, 215

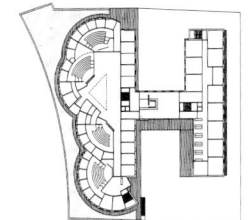

ESADE Building
Carretera de Esplugues. Barcelona
Competition
Not executed
1989

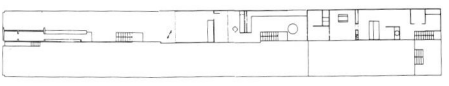
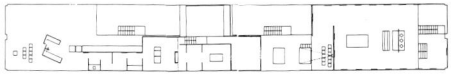

"Josep María Jujol, arquitecte" Exhibition Assembly
Organisers: COAC and the Centre Georges Pompidou
Barcelona (1988), Tarragona, Lérida and Gerona (1989) COAC
MOPU Exhibition Gallery in Madrid (1990). Centre Georges Pompidou in Paris (1990)

Bibliography: 13, 19, 32, 209

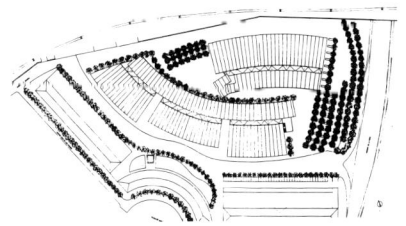
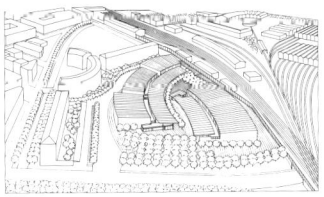

Industrial Park and Shopping Mall in Vilanova i la Geltrú
"La Sinía de les vaques", Vilanova i la Geltrú. Barcelona
INCASOL, Catalonian Regional Govt.
Not executed
1990

Adaptation of the Annexe to the Barcelona History Museum
Veguer c/v Llibretería. Barcelona
Barcelona City Council
1989-1991
Surveyor: Jaume Martí Almestoy
Fittings and equipment: O.I.T.
Construction: Sapic, s.a.
Built surface area: 1,981 m²

Bibliography: 195

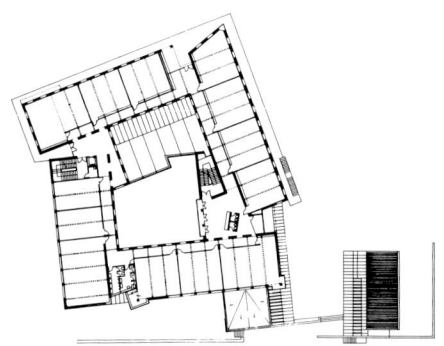

Secondary School in Gironella
Pons de les Eres s/n
Gironella. Barcelona
Catalonian Regional Government
With Pere Fontdevila, architect
Surveyor: Jaume Martí Almestoy
Structures: Robert Brufau
Construction: Construcciones
Generales Roca, s.l.
Built surface area: 4,635 m²

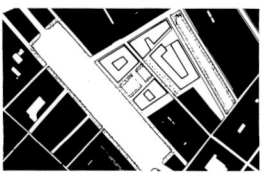

City Block Distribution in the Raval Quarter
Barcelona
Barcelona City Council
Competition, not executed, 1990

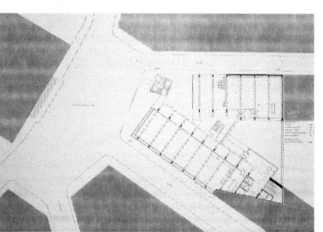

Tarrasa Central Library
Plaça de l'Estació del Nord
Tarrasa. Barcelona
Tarrasa Town Council
First design, not executed
1991

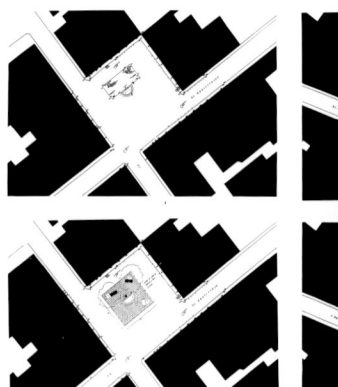
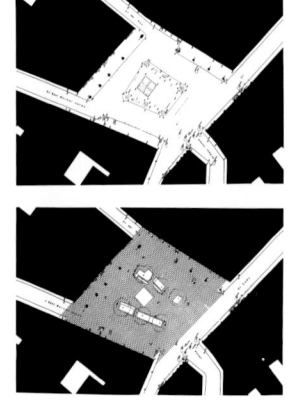
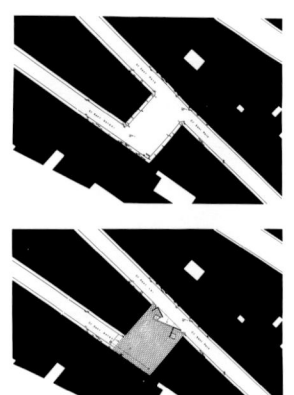

Development of Three Town Squares in Vilaseca
Plaça de les Creus, Plaça de les Voltes, Plaça de Sant Esteve
Vilaseca. Tarragona
Vilaseca Town Council
1990-1991
Surveyor: Municipal Technical Services

Refurbishment and Restoration of the Sant Sadurní d'Anoia Town Hall
Sant Sadurní d'Anoia. Barcelona
Not executed
1991

Detached House in Can Caralleu
Capella de Can Caralleu 12. Barcelona
1991-1993
Surveyor: Jaume Martí Almestoy
Construction: Pedro Asensio, s.a.
Site surface area: 1,000 m²

Bibliography: 52, 123, 146, 172, 201

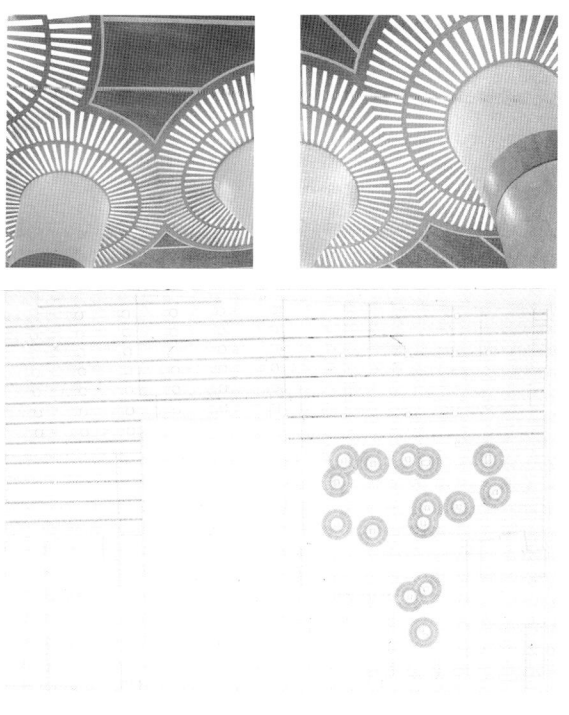

Site Adaptation for the CTNE Telephone Exchange Offices
Sant Jaume c/v General Manso
Sant Feliú de Llobregat. Barcelona
1988-1991
Surveyor: Jaume Martí Almestoy
Construction: Lluis Casas, s.a.
Built surface area: 1,880 m²

Bibliography: 36, 145

Refurbishment and Restoration of the Metropol Theatre
Rambla Nova 46. Tarragona
Tarragona City Council
1992-1995
Collaborating architect: Joan Vera
Surveyor: Jaume Martí Almestoy
Structures: Robert Brufau
Fittings and equipment: Instal.lacions Arquitectòniques
Stagehouse: Santi Serrate
Acoustics: Higini Arau
Construction: Fomento de Construcciones y Contratas, s.a.
Built surface area: 2,625 m²

Bibliography: 10, 41, 92, 110, 138, 147, 152, 163, 183, 184, 207

Housing Block in Vallcarca
Sant Eudald 16-18. Barcelona
First design: 1991
Second design: 1991-1992
Execution: 1993-1996
Surveyor: Jaume Martí Almestoy
Structures: Robert Brufau
Construction: Catalana d'Obres, s.a.

Bibliography: 122, 173, 203

Detached House in Colonia Güell
Claudio Güell 18
Santa Coloma de Cerelló. Barcelona
1991-1994
Surveyor: Jaume Martí Almestoy
Structures: Robert Brufau
Construction: Germans Font
Built surface area: 200 m²

Bibliography: 149, 161, 171, 202

Administration Building for the Computer Science School
Module B2. Campus Nord
Universidad Politécnica de Barcelona
Barcelona
1993-1995
Surveyor: Jaume Martí Almestoy
Structures: Robert Brufau
Fittings and equipment: Instal.lacions Arquitectòniques
Construction: Construcciones San José s.a. and Dragados y Construcciones, s.a.
Built surface area: 2,300 m²

Bibliography: 106, 143, 181, 218

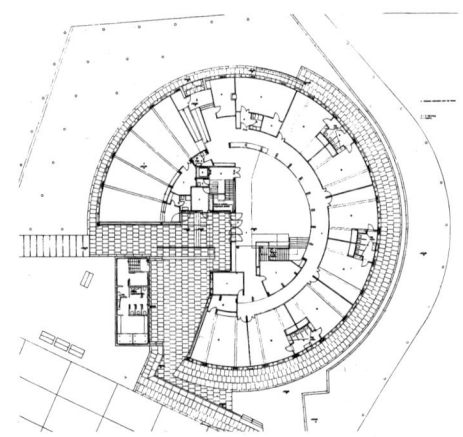

Collblanc Primary School
Collblanc 136. Barcelona
Second design: 1992-1996
Surveyor: Jaume Casas
Structures: Robert Brufau
School fittings: J. Comas
Carpark fittings: Instal.lacions Arquitectòniques
Construction: Movilma, Teyco
School built surface area: 3,434 m²
Carpark built surface area: 7,090 m²

Bibliography: 17, 49, 115

Housing Block (with 28 apartments) in Calle Carme
Carme 55-57, Roig 28-36. Barcelona
Procivesa
1992-1995
Surveyor: Jaume Martí Almestoy
Structures: Robert Brufau
Construction: Contratas y Obras, s.a.
Built surface area: 3,996 m²

Bibliography: 40, 110, 119, 121, 136, 140, 142, 162, 164, 176, 182, 185, 204, 206, 214

Lecture Rooms and Bar for the Law School
Pedralbes Campus
Universidad Central de Barcelona
1993-1996
Surveyor: Jaume Martí Almestoy
Structures: OFEP
Fittings: Instal.lacions Arquitectòniques
Construction: OCP, Dragados y Construcciones, s.a. and Rubau, s.a.
Built surface area: 4,773 m²

Bibliography: 105

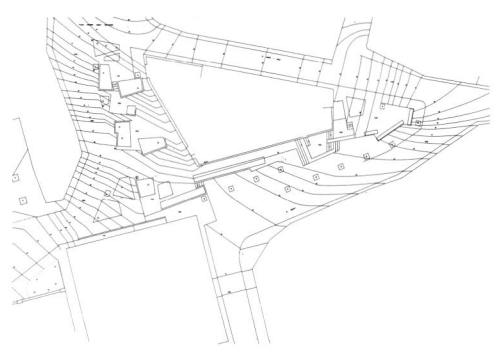

Remodelling Work on the Old Quarter of Pallejà
Plaça Mossen Jacint Verdaguer and Plaça Mayor surrounding areas
Pallejà. Barcelona.
Barcelona Metropolitan Area
1994-1995
Surveyors: Jordi Ardévol and Manel Sans
Fittings: J. Bayo
Construction: Construcciones Navás

Bibliography: 47, 205

Secondary School in Torredembarra
Av. Sant Jordi 62
Torredembarra. Tarragona
Catalonian Regional Government
1993-1996
Surveyor: Jaume Martí Almestoy
Structures: Robert Brufau
Fittings: Lola Queralt
Construction: Vicsan, s.a.
Site surface area: 10,080 m²
Built surface area: 5,255 m²

Bibliography: 111, 148, 150, 208

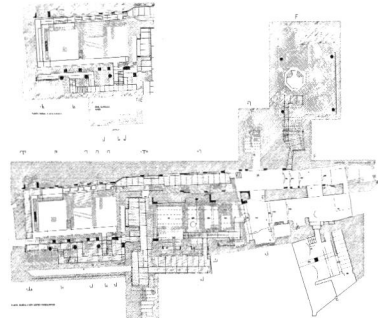

Adaptation of the Comtes-Plaça Sant Iu Underground Storey of the Barcelona History Museum
Barcelona
Barcelona City Council
1994-1995
Surveyor: Jaume Martí Almestoy
Fittings: JG y Asociados
Construction: Closa Alegret, s.a.

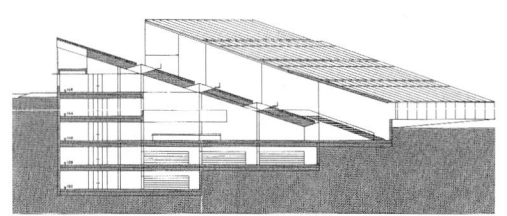

Central Library for the Universidad Autónoma de Barcelona
Plaça Cívica
Universidad Autónoma de Barcelona
Bellaterra. Barcelona
Competition, not executed
1995

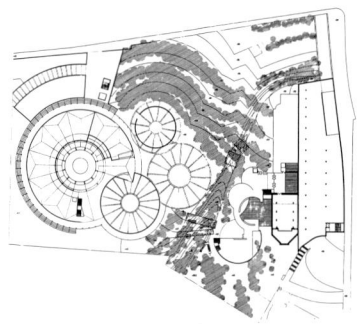

Extension to the Science Museum
Teodor Roviralta 55. Barcelona
Caixa d'Estalvis de Catalunya
Competition, not executed
1995

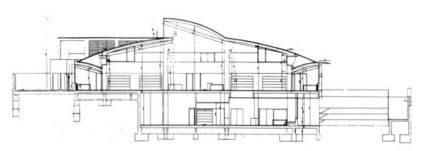

Tarrasa Central Library
Sant Gaietà 94.
Tarrasa. Barcelona
Design executed: 1995-1997
Surveyor: Jaume Martí Almestoy
Structures: Robert Brufau
Fittings: JG y Asociados
Construction: Ferrovial, s.a.
Built surface area: 3,504 m²

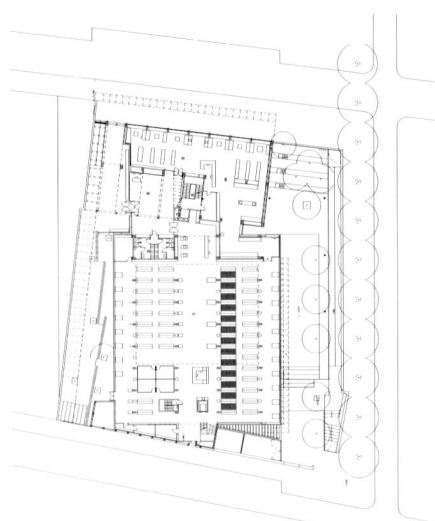
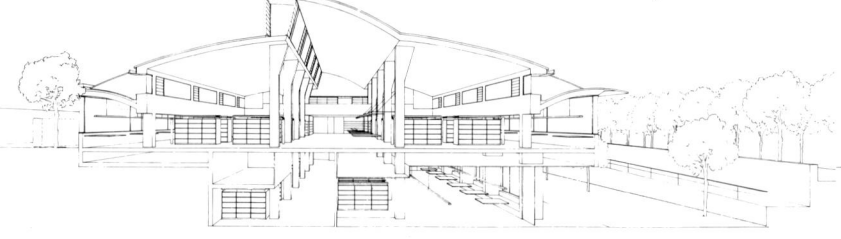

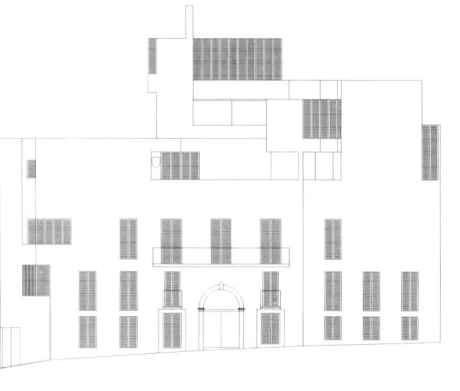
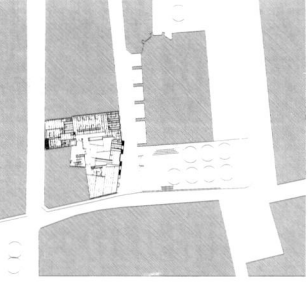

Vilaseca Town Hall
Plaça de l'Esglesia
Vilaseca. Tarragona
Design: 1995-1996
Design executed: 1996
Surveyor: Jaume Martí Almestoy
Structures: Robert Brufau
Fittings: JG y Asociados
Built surface area: 2,331 m²

Three Detached Buildings and One Housing-and-Shops Block in Conegliano
Former Zanussi Industrial Park
Conegliano. Italy
Conegliano Iniziative Immobiliari, s.a.
Design: 1995-1996
Works scheduled to begin: 1997

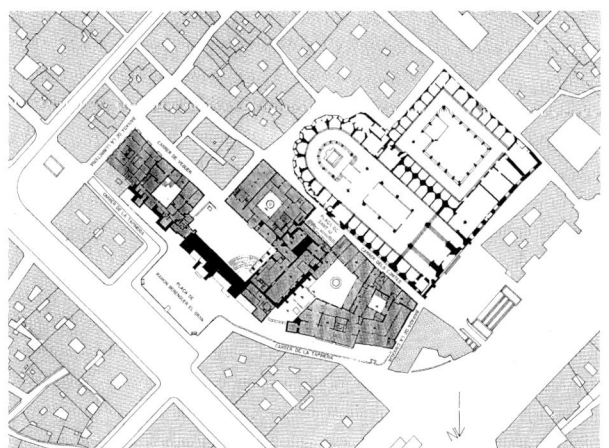

Distribution of the Barcelona History Museum Building Complex
Barcelona City Council
Works in execution: 1997

Marés Museum Distribution
Barcelona
Barcelona City Council
Works in execution: 1997

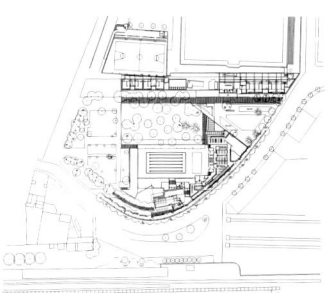

"Fondo d'en Peixo" Park Distribution and Municipal Swimming Pool Remodelling
Avenida del Canal / Calle Penedés
El Prat de Llobregat. Barcelona
El Prat de Llobregat Town Council
Works in execution: 1997

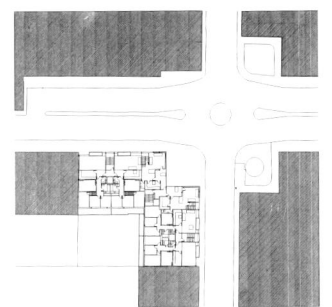 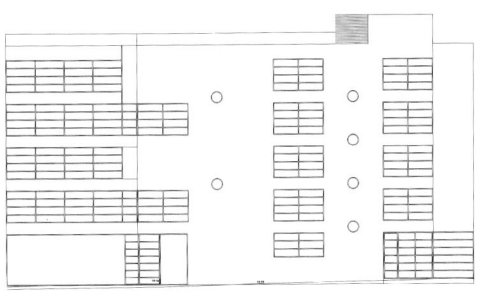

Housing Block (with 28 apartments) in Gavà
Gavà. Barcelona
Plaça de la Font Groga
GTI Gavanenca de Terrenys i Inmobles, Gavà Town Council
Works in execution: 1997

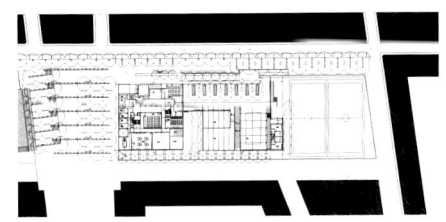

School in Tarrasa
Tarrasa. Barcelona
Cervantes c/v Pantà
Catalonian Regional Government
Works in execution: 1997

Building Alterations for a Block of Housing and Shops in Sant Feliú de Llobregat
Paseo Nadal 24-26
Sant Feliú de Llobregat. Barcelona
Works in execution: 1997

Biography

1945 Llinás was born in Castellón de la Plana.

1962-1969 Studies architecture at the Escuela Técnica Superior de Arquitectura in Barcelona.

1969 Graduates from the Escuela Técnica Superior de Arquitectura in Barcelona.

Josep Llinás Carmona
Avda. República Argentina 62, 08023 Barcelona, Spain
Tel. (34 3) 212 37 14, Fax (34 3) 417 65 69

Collaborators 1969-1996
Jaume Martí Almestoy, surveyor, permanent collaborator since 1980. Joan Vera García, architect, permanent collaborator since 1990.

Carlos Llinás Carmona, architect. Eva Monte Hevia, architect. Lolita Queralt Gimeno, architect. Structure calculations: Robert Brufau i Niubo, and occasionally OFEP: Joaquim Pascual. V. Martí, J. Camps, architects. Instal.lacions Arquitectòniques, S.L. and JG & Asociados, fittings and installations calculations. Antonio Foraster Mariscal, architect. Arturo Freddiani Sarfati, architect. Carles Giribert Sanllehy, architect. Alex Llarch, Alfonsina Ortega González and Isa Sebastián Perruca, secretaries.

Albert Vidal Pericás, Fina Royo Abelló, Josep Buscato, Joan Lluis Casajoana, Are Olivar, Carlos Llinás, Armand Fernández Prat, Cinto Oms, José Adriao, Magda Llinás Bisbal, César González Valdivieso, Mar Raventós, Joan Vera García, Eva Monte Hevia, Pedro Pablo Vaquer, Jorge Sánchez, David Portoles, Dori Castellá Daga, Pablo Carbo Bechtold, Jordi Duatis, Mª Antonia Mayol, Elizabeth Font, José Palomero, Isabel Martínez, Bernardo Luna, Federico Longo, Claudio Spagnotto, Sergio Cánovas Paradell, Nadia Casabella Alvarez, Silvia Contreras López, Pedro Cortacans, Antonio Jansana, Guillem Costa Calsamiglia, Moisés Puente Rodríguez, Inés Rivera Marinello, Mónica Rozman, Elena Vives, Xavier Rovira Ricart, Diego Santamaría Gómez, Clara Jiménez Xiberta, Ton Llopart Cirilo, Jordi Mercadé Rogel, Imanol Montero Viar, Xavier Osarte i Salvany, Pedro Pacheco, Oriol Parés Camps, Claudia Thomet, Joao Costa Cavaca, Christoph Antesberger, Christiane Hops, Cristóbal Fernández, Anna Costal Costa, Doris Agotai, Anna Gener Esteve, Mikel Astiazaran Goñi, Margarita Jover Biboum, Xavier Gracia Quílez, Maurice Custers, Eloy Parrales Zapico, Esther Pitarch Sales, Yolanda Nadal Campistrou, Architecture students.

Academic Experience

1970-1989 Lecturer, Project Design Department, Escuela Técnica Superior de Arquitectura de Barcelona.

1978-1981 Assistant Professor, Project Design II Course, Escuela Técnica Superior de Arquitectura de Barcelona.

1983-1991 Head Professor, Project Design V Course, Escuela Técnica Superior de Arquitectura del Vallès, Barcelona.

1991 Speaker, *Arquitectura de Bibliotecas - Library Architecture* Seminar, Lisbon.

1992 Tutoring Professor, I Architecture Workshop, II Biennale of Architecture, Universidad Internacional Menéndez y Pelayo, Santander.

1993 Professor at the Summer Workshop organised by Haus der Architektur, Graz, Austria.

1994 Professor at the Summer Workshop organised by the Architektur Zentrum Wien, Vienna.

1996 Speaker, *Habitar la Ciudad - City Life* Summer Course, Universidad Complutense de Madrid, Aguadulce (Almería).

Speaker, International Design Seminar, Barcelona, organised by the School of Architecture of the Universidad Javeriana de Bogotá (Colombia) and the Universidad Politécnica de Cataluña.

Professor, *La Memoria del Lugar - Memory of the Place* Summer Workshop, organised by the Cultural Department of the Colegio de Arquitectos de Baleares, Mallorca Delegation.

Publications by Josep Llinás

"Un plan para el peu del funicular", *Boletín Informativo del Ayuntamiento de Barcelona*, Barcelona, 1981.

"Sobre la fotografía de una niña en la casa Farnsworth", *Quaderns*, Barcelona, 1982, nº 152, pp. 40-41.
— *José Llinás. Obras y proyectos 1976-1985*, exhibition catalogue, Colegio Oficial de Arquitectos de Madrid, Madrid, 1985, pp. 17-20.

"Josep María Jujol", *El País*, Sunday supplement, Barcelona, 11 December 1983.
— *SD*, nº 9, Tokyo, 1988, pp. 75-90.

"Josep María Jujol, architectus 1879-1949", *Quaderns*, nº 163, Barcelona, 1984, pp.98-101.
— *José Llinás. Obras y proyectos 1976-1985* exhibition catalogue, Colegio Oficial de Arquitectos de Madrid, Madrid, 1985.
— *SITES*, nº 14, New York, 1986, pp. 40-41.

"Arquitectura racional", *José Llinás. Obras y proyectos 1976-1985*, exhibition catalogue, Colegio Oficial de Arquitectos de Madrid, Madrid, 1985, pp.15 16.

"Sobre la relativa importancia de la forma", *2C. Construccion de la ciudad*, nº 22, Barcelona, 1985, pp. 24-25.

"Coderch, una dimensión ética", *Boletín informativo de la UPC*, Barcelona, 1985.
— *Homenatge a J. A. Coderch de Sentmenat*, exhibition catalogue, Direcció General d'Arquitectura i Habitatge, Generalitat de Catalunya, Barcelona, 1988, p. 238.

"Si como creo ...", *Quaderns*, nº 169-170, Barcelona, 1986, pp. 96-97.

"Jujol, una insólita capacidad para detener el tiempo", *Barcelona, Metrópolis Mediterránea*, nº 2, Ayuntamiento de Barcelona, Barcelona, 1986, pp. 113-116.
— *Josep Mª Jujol, architecte 1879-1949*, exhibition catalogue, Centre Georges Pompidou, Paris, 1991, pp. 6-15.

"Mies, la fundación de una técnica", *Arquitectura*, nº 267, Colegio Oficial de Arquitectos de Madrid, Madrid, 1987, pp. 44-53.

"El Gobierno Civil de Tarragona", *Quaderns*, nº 172, Barcelona, 1987, pp. 104-105.

"Josep María Jujol a Sant Joan Despí", introduction to *Josep Mª Jujol a Sant Joan Despí. Projectes i obra 1913-1949*, Montserrat Duran i Albaneda, Xavier Miserachs (photographs), Corporación Metropolitana de Barcelona, Barcelona, 1987, pp. 11-12.
— *Quaderns*, nº 179-180, Barcelona, 1989, pp. 60-63.

"Nada por aquí, nada por allá ...", prologue to *Alejandro de la Sota*, by Alejandro de la Sota, Pronaos, Madrid, 1990, p. 11.

Josep Llinás, Jordi Sarrá (photographs), *Josep María Jujol*, Taschen, Cologne, 1992.

"Confundir al cliente", house presentation: detached house in Can Caralleu, detached house in Vallcarca and detached house in Colonia Güell, *Arquitectos*, nº 132, Consejo Superior de los Colegios de Arquitectos de España, Madrid, 1994, pp. 66-67.

"Construir en Ciutat Vella", *El Periódico*, Barcelona, 11 February 1995, p. 42.

"Deshacer y construir", *Quaderns*, nº 203, Barcelona, 1995, p. 39.

"Las aguas mansas son profundas", *Quaderns*, nº 212, Barcelona, 1996. p. 140.

"Un fracaso esplendoroso", reflections on the K. Melnikov house; Alday, Iñaki; Martínez Lapeña, J. Antonio; Moneo, Rafael: *Aprendiendo de todas sus casas*, for the series *Textos i Documents d'Arquitectura*, nº 3, ETSAV and Edicions UPC, Sant Cugat del Vallés, 1996, p.58.

"Mejor despeinado", *Jujol recuperat*, exhibition catalogue, Colegio de Arquitectos de Cataluña. Demarcación de Tarragona, Tarragona, 1996, pp. 12-16.
— *Quaderns*, nº 212, Barcelona, 1996, p. 141.

"Solidaridad entre desconocidos", article for the monograph on Alvaro Siza, Tanais Ediciones, s.a., Seville (in the press).

Conferences and Roundtables

1983 "K. Melnikov", conference, Escuela de Arquitectura del Vallès, Sant Cugat del Vallés, Barcelona.

1984 "La fundación de una técnica", conference, doctorate course and conference cycle on Mies Van der Rohe, Colegio Oficial de Arquitectos de Barcelona and Escuela de Arquitectura de Madrid.
Participant in the Montjuïc Olympic Ring Draft Competition roundtables, Colegio Oficial de Arquitectos de Gerona and Colegio Oficial de Arquitectos de Madrid.

1985 "Josep María Jujol, arquitecto", conference, Colegio Oficial de Arquitectos de Madrid.
"El Gobierno Civil de Tarragona", Galería de Arquitectura, C.R.C., Barcelona.

1986 "La arquitectura detenida en la construcción", conference, first centenary of the birth of Mies Van der Rohe, Colegio Oficial de Arquitectos de Madrid.

1987 "Josep María Jujol, arquitecto", conference, Colegio Oficial de Arquitectos de Tarragona.

1988 Roundtable on the work of J.A. Coderch, Colegio Oficial de Arquitectos de Barcelona.

1991 Roundtable on architecture journals, Colegio Oficial de Arquitectos de Granada.

1992 *Habitatge i context urbà a l'arquitectura catalana*, book presentation, Barcelona.

1995 "Jujol recuperat", conference on Jujol's work (Metropol Theatre), Colegio Oficial de Arquitectos de Tarragona.

1996 Lecturer at the III International Seminar on Catalonian Architecture, *La crisis de la ciudad Latinoamericana - Crisis of the Latin American City*, organised by the Pontificia Universidad Javeriana, Bogotá (Colombia).
Roundtable on Alejandro de la Sota, "Conversaciones en torno a Alejandro de la Sota", Escuela Técnica Superior de Arquitectura de Madrid.
Roundtable on Alejandro de la Sota, Colegio Oficial de Arquitectos de Tarragona.
Roundtable on architecture competitions, Universidad de Alicante and Escuela Técnica Superior de Arquitectura de Valencia.

Roundtable at the Interacció '96 Seminar, *Equipaments: instruments o monuments?*, organised by the Centro de Estudios y Recursos Culturales and the Barcelona Provincial Council. Lecturer at the *El proyecto en la transformación de la ciudad* Seminar, organised by the Colegio de Arquitectos de Andalucía Oriental, Málaga delegation.

Member of the Jury in Architecture Competitions

1987 Best ideas competition for the distribution of a park in the Castell de Rubí area.

1988 Europan, international best ideas competition on housing subjects.
Best ideas competition for the design of a civic centre for the Rondilla quarter, Valladolid.
Best ideas competition for the distribution of the San Agustín barracks, Barcelona City Council.
Vizcaya Award, Colegio de Arquitectos Vasco-Navarro.

1989 Best ideas competition for the distribution of the pedestrian precinct in Mahón's town centre and rehabilitation of the Plaza Esplanada square, Mahón (Menorca).

1990 Competition for the new headquarters of the Colegio Oficial de Arquitectos de Lérida.
Colegio Oficial de Arquitectos de Valencia Award, 1988-89.

1992 Head office for the Vic Delegation of the Colegio Oficial de Arquitectos de Cataluña.
Draft competition for the development of the Rambla de Mataró, Mataró Town Council.
Grand Prix National d'Architecture 1992, Paris.

1993 Soluciones Constructivas Pladur III National Award.
Consultant at the II Biennale of Spanish Architecture.

1994 1992-93 Architecture Award, Colegio Oficial de Arquitectos de Oviedo.
Draft competition for the Tortosa Exhibition Hall.
Best ideas competition for the rehabilitation and adaptation of the mansion on Calle Recoletas to house the head office of the Colegio Oficial de Arquitectos de Asturias, in Gijón.

1995 Best ideas competition to remodel the Plaça Major square in Prades.

Competition for the design and execution of the Chemical Technology Centre of the Universidad de Alicante.
Draft competition for the new head office of the Reial Club Nàutic nautical club in Tarragona.

1996 Patronat de l'Habitatge competition, Tarragona.
Competition for the rehabilitation of the Son Espanyol houses, in Palma de Mallorca.

Awards

1977 FAD Interior Design Award, 1976, for shop premises in Barcelona.

1990 Villa de Madrid Architecture and Town Planning Award for the "Josep María Jujol, arquitecto" exhibition, organised by the Colegio de Arquitectos de Cataluña.

1996 Ciutat de Barcelona 1995 Architecture and Town Planning Award for the housing block on Carme/Roig streets.
Rehabitec 1996 Building Award, sponsored by the Catalonian Regional Government and organised by ITEC, for the restoration and rehabilitation of the Metropol Theatre in Tarragona.
FAD 1996 Architecture Award for the restoration and rehabilitation of the Metropol Theatre in Tarragona.
Dragados y Construcciones 1996 Spanish Architecture Award, CEOE Foundation, Madrid, for the apartment building on Calle Carme, Barcelona, *ex aequo* with the Madrid Community Sports Stadium, designed by Cruz/Ortiz.

Exhibitions

1980 *Arquitectura catalana*, Catalonian Regional Government, at the Centre George Pompidou, Paris.

1981 *Catalunya avui*, Catalonian Regional Government, at the Unesco head office, Paris.

1982 *Obra pública en Cataluña, 1850-1982, Barcelona*, Catalonian Regional Government.

1983 *Arquitectura racional, revista 2c*, Barcelona (travelling exhibition).

1984 *Els centres sanitaris de la Generalitat*, Barcelona and Mallorca.

1985 *Josep Llinás. Obras y proyectos, 1976-1985*, Colegio Oficial de Arquitectos de Madrid.
30 oeuvres d'architecture espagnole, Europalia 85, Ministry of Culture, Brussels.

1986 *Arquitectura catalana*, Catalonian Regional Government.
Arquitectura. Obra pública en Catalunya 1980-85, Catalonian Regional Government and Colegio Oficial de Arquitectos de Cataluña.

1988 *L'architecture, le lieu et la mémoire*, French Academy: Rome, Lisbon, Paris.
Barcelona 92, Barcelona City Council, Barcelona.

1989 *Luoghi d'architettura europea*, Academia di Francia a Roma, Rome; Fondaçao Gulbenkian, Lisbon; Maison de l'Architecture, Paris.

1990 *Discursos sobre arquitectura*, School of Architecture, Oporto.
Catalan Architecture, University of Waterloo, Canada.

1991 *Itineraris d'arquitectura catalana*, Colegio Oficial de Arquitectos de Barcelona.
São Paulo Biennale of Art, under the Pavilion of Belgium, São Paulo, Brazil.
I Muestra de diez años de arquitectura española 1980-90, Ministry of Public Works and Town Planning, Madrid.
José Llinás, 1976-1989, exhibition/presentation of issue no.14 of *Documentos de Arquitectura*, Almería and Barcelona.

1992 *4 de Barcelona* (Torres/Lapeña, E. Miralles, José Luis Mateo and Josep Llinás), Arc en Rêve Centre d'Architecture, Bordeaux, France.
Projectes per la Barcelona del 93, Colegio Oficial de Arquitectos de Barcelona.
Muestra de arquitectura: la vivienda unifamiliar en Menorca, Colegio Oficial de Arquitectos de Baleares.
4 de Barcelona, Centre d'Expositions Ville du Parc, Annemasse, France.

1993 *A New Generation of Spanish Architecture*, Architectural Association School of Architecture, London.
Cataluña: arquitectura contemporánea, School of Architecture and Town Planning, Universidad de Santiago de Chile.
Josep Llinás. Obra propia. Haus der Architecktur, Graz, Austria.

1994 *The wide space*, Architektur Zentrum Wien, Vienna.

1995 *Minimal*: Ivan Kroupa, Simón Ungers, J. Llinás, Rom Gallery, Oslo, Sweden.
III Bienal de Arquitectura española 1993-1994, Ministry of Public Works, Transport and the Environment, Consejo Superior de Colegios de Arquitectos de España, Universidad Internacional Menéndez y Pelayo, Santander.

1996 *Arquitectura a Catalunya 1977-96. 20 anys de democracia*. XIX International Architecture Congress (IAU), Catalonian Regional Government.
Premios de Urbanismo, Arquitectura y Obra Pública del Ayuntamiento de Madrid, Madrid City Council, City Planning Municipal Office.
In Quebec, Canada. Catalonian Regional Government, Teaching Department.
Arquigrafies, Centre Cívic Pati Llimona, Barcelona City Council, Barcelona.
Arquitectura de autor, Pamplona Higher Technical School of Architecture, Universidad de Navarra.

Conferences on his work

1981 Juan de la Rosa Institute, Madrid.

1982 Project Design IV Course, Escuela de Arquitectura, Barcelona.

1984 Colegio de Arquitectos de Cantabria, Santander.

1985 Colegio de Arquitectos de Madrid.
Colegio de Arquitectos de Tarragona.
Ecole d'Architecture UP8, Paris.
Colegio de Arquitectos de Aragón, Zaragoza.
Colegio de Arquitectos de Canarias, Las Palmas, Tenerife.

1986 Escuela de Arquitectura de Valladolid.
Colegio de Arquitectos de Barcelona.
Colegio de Arquitectos de Gerona.

1987 Colegio de Arquitectos de Andalucía Oriental, Almería.
The Architectural Association, London.
Colegio de Arquitectos, Vitoria-Gasteiz.
Colegio de Arquitectos de Tarragona.

1988 Colegio de Arquitectos de Valencia.
Escuela de Arquitectura de La Coruña.
Colegio de Arquitectos Vasco-Navarro, Bilbao.
The Polytechnic North, London.

1989 Antonio Machado Summer University, Baeza (Jaén).

La Arquitectura, el lugar y la memoria, Fundaçao Gulbenkian, Lisbon.
Architectural Heritage Refurbishing Works Course, Colegio de Arquitectos de Barcelona.
V Seminar on Architectural Heritage Refurbishing Works, Colegio de Arquitectos de La Rioja.

1990 *La protección del patrimonio arquitectónico del siglo XX*, The European Council.
Oporto Professional College of Architects, Portugal.
Nueva arquitectura española, ETSAV and COA, Valladolid.
Arquitectura contemporánea, Colegio de Arquitectos de Alicante.
Ecole d'Architecture UP8, Paris.

1991 Escuela Técnica Superior de Arquitectura de Navarra.
Colegio de Arquitectos Vasco-Navarro, Pamplona.
Escuela de Arquitectura de Las Palmas.
Arquitectura de bibliotecas, seminar, Lisbon.
Arquitectura española actual, Escuela Técnica Superior de Arquitectura de Barcelona.
Escuela Técnica Superior de Arquitectutra de Valencia.
Colegio de Arquitectos de Gerona.
Ecole d'Architecture de Bordeaux, France.

1992 Colegio Oficial de Arquitectos de Las Palmas de Gran Canaria.
Colegio de Arquitectos de Barcelona.
Juan de la Rosa Institute, Colegio Mayor San Juan Evangelista, Madrid.
Project Design IV Course, Escuela Técnica Superior de Arquitectura de Barcelona.
Escuela de Arquitectura del Valles.

1993 Project Design IV Course, Escuela Técnica Superior de Arquitectura de Barcelona.
Three conferences during the 1992-93 year, Escuela Técnica Superior de Arquitectura de Barcelona.
Actuaciones en Ciutat Vella en Barcelona, part of the *Intervenciones en centros históricos* summer course, Complutense de Almería, Almería.
Spanish Biennale of Architecture 1991-1992.
Colegio de Arquitectos de Asturias.
La pequeña dimensión course, Universidad Menéndez y Pelayo, Santander.
Museu d'Història de la Ciutat de Barcelona.

1994 Escuela Técnica Superior de Arquitectura de Barcelona, on the Spanish Embassy in Paris.

1995 Ecole d'Architecture de Bretagne, Rennes.

Escuela Técnica Superior de Arquitectura de Barcelona.
Colegio de Arquitectos de León.
Casa de una planta en la Colonia Güell. Santa Coloma de Cervelló.
SPAU (Seminario Permanente de Arquitectura Urbana) Association, Colegio de Arquitectos de Málaga.
Haus Der Architektur, Graz, Austria.
Architektur Zentrum Wien, Vienna.
Colegio de Arquitectos de Tarragona.
ETH (Eidegnössische Technische Hochschule), Zurich, Switzerland.

1996 *Construir en Ciutat Vella*, seminar, Escuela de Arquitectura de Barcelona.
La Reforma del Teatro Metropol, Heritage Commission, Colegio de Arquitectos de Cataluña.
Arquitectura española, cycle, Colegio de Arquitectos de Aragón, Zaragoza Delegation.
III Seminario Internacional de Arquitectura Catalana, Bogotá and Medellín (Colombia).
Edificios en cascos urbanos, Escuela Técnica Superior de Arquitectura de Barcelona.
Arquitecturas de autor, Escuela Técnica Superior de Arquitectura de Pamplona, Universidad de Navarra.
Habitar la ciudad, course, Universidad Complutense de Madrid, Aguadulce (Almería).
III Curso sobre intervención en el paisaje y en el espacio urbano, Gerona.
1996 Contemporary Architecture, cycle, Centro Cultural Parque de España, Rosario (Argentina).
Architetture per la città, cycle, Istituto Nazionale d'Architettura (IN/ARCH), Brescia.
EINA School, Barcelona, on the Metropol Theatre.
Escuela Técnica Superior de Arquitectura de Barcelona, on Llinás's complete works.

Bibliography

Books

[1]. Atrium (Ed.): *Architectural Houses: Casas en el mar*, Atrium, Barcelona, 1991, pp. 128-140.
[2]. — *Architectural Houses: Casas en la ciudad*, Atrium, Barcelona, 1991, pp. 86-93.

[3]. Ayuntamiento de Barcelona: *Plans i projectes per a Barcelona 1981-82*, Ayuntamiento de Barcelona, Area de Urbanismo, Barcelona, 1983, pp. 217-218.

[4]. Baldellou, Miguel A.; Capitel, Antón: *Summa artis. Historia general del arte. XL. Arquitectura española del siglo XX*, Espasa Calpe, Madrid, 1995, p. 496.
[5]. — p. 583.

[6]. Bohigas, Oriol; Buchanan, Peter; Magnago Lampugnani, V.: *Barcelona, arquitectura y ciudad, 1980-92*, Gustavo Gili, Barcelona, 1990, pp. 40-45.

[7]. Brú, Eduard; Mateo, José Luis: *Arquitectura española contemporánea. Spanish Contemporary Architecture*, Gili, Barcelona, 1984, p. 11.
[8]. — *Arquitectura europea contemporánea*, Gustavo Gili, Barcelona, 1987, pp. 60-63.

[9]. Colegio Oficial de Arquitectos de Catalunya: *Guia d'arquitectura de Menorca*, COAC, Barcelona, 1980, p. 62.
[10]. — *Guia d'arquitectura del camp,* Tarragona, 1995, pp. 230-231.
[11]. — p. 241.
[12]. — pp. 273, 275.
[13]. — *Imatges 1988-1990*, catalogue, COAC, Barcelona, 1990, p. 5.
[14]. — *Itineraris d'arquitectura catalana, 1984-1991*, catalogue, Quaderns, Barcelona, 1991, p. 46.
[15]. — pp. 108-109.

[16]. Colegio Oficial de Arquitectos de Andalucía Oriental: *Documentos de arquitectura*, nº 11, COAAO, Almería, 1990, pp. 5-18.
[17]. — pp. 19-30.
[18]. — pp. 31-36.
[19]. — pp. 37-40.
[20]. — pp. 41-46.
[21]. — pp. 47-50.
[22]. — pp. 51-58.
[23]. — pp. 59-60.
[24]. — pp. 61-68.
[25]. — pp. 69-78.
[26]. — pp. 79-82.
[27]. — pp. 83-84.
[28]. — pp. 85-88.
[29]. — pp. 89-91.

[30]. Corporació Metropolitana de Barcelona: *Projectar la ciutat metropolitana*, Corporació Metropolitana de Barcelona, Barcelona, 1980.

[31]. Costafreda, Mercè: *El Col.legi d'Arquitectes a Tarragona*, Colegio Oficial de Arquitectos de Cataluña, Delegación de Tarragona, Tarragona, 1992, pp. 121.
[32]. — p. 123-125.

[33]. Diputació de Barcelona: *50 aniversari del Museu Arqueológic*, catalogue, Diputació de Barcelona, Barcelona, 1986, pp. 116-119.
[34]. — *Revista de museus*, Diputació de Barcelona, 1987, pp. 57-59.
[35]. — *L'obra a fer*, Diputació de Barcelona, 1987, pp. 129-143.

[36]. Diseño Interior (Ed.): *Monografía. Oficinas*, Diseño Interior, Madrid, 1991, pp. 60-65.

[37]. El Croquis (Ed.): *1888-1991. Premio Nacional de Arquitectura de ladrillo,* El Croquis, Madrid, 1992, pp. 13-15.

[38]. Fernández Alba, Angel (Exhibition Commissar), Ministerio de Obras Públicas y Urbanismo: *Architecture Espagnole. Trente Oeuvres. Années 50-Années 80/Spaanse Architectuur. Jaren'50-Jaren'80*, exhibition catalogue, Europalia, Brussels, 1985, Dirección General de Arquitectura y Vivienda, Ministerio de Obras Públicas y Urbanismo, Madrid, 1985, pp. 138-141.

[39]. Flores, Carlos; Güell, Xavier: *Guía de arquitectura de España 1929-1996*, Fundación Caja de Arquitectos, Barcelona, 1996, p. 110.
[40]. — p. 132.
[41]. — p. 277.
[42]. — p. 278.

[43]. Frampton, Kenneth (Introduction); Campo Baeza, Alberto; Poisay, Charles: *Young Spanish Architecture*, Colegio Oficial de Arquitectos de Madrid, Universidad Politécnica de Madrid, 1985, p. 114.
[44]. — p. 114.
[45]. — p. 115.
[46]. — p. 116.
[47]. — p. 116.
[48]. — p. 117.

[49]. Frampton, Kenneth (Introduction); Collova, Roberto (photographs): *Luoghi d'architettura europea*, Carte Segete, Rome, 1989, pp. 54-59.

[50]. Frampton, Kenneth; Capitel, Antón; Pérez Escolano, Víctor; Solà-Morales, Ignasi de: *España: Arquitecturas de hoy*, Ministerio de Obras Públicas y Transportes, Madrid, 1992, p. 34.
[51]. — pp. 35-36, 56.

[52]. Frechilla, Javier; Carreras Moysi, Borja; Duró i Pifarré, Jaime; Lluch, Ernest; Bonell, Esteve; Campo, Alberto; Gallego, José M.; Mangado, Francisco J. (Selection Committee and Jury): *III Bienal de Arquitectura Española. 3rd Biennial*

Spanish Architecture, Ministerio de Obras Públicas, Transportes y Medio Ambiente, Consejo Superior de Colegios de Arquitectos de España, Universidad Internacional Menéndez y Pelayo, Madrid, 1991, pp. 112-115.

[53]. Gausa, Manel; Cervelló, Marta: *Guía de arquitectura contemporánea. Barcelona y su área territorial, 1928-1990*, Quaderns, Barcelona, 1991, p. 15.
[54]. — p. 24.
[55]. — p. 31.
[56]. — p. 67.
[57]. — p. 99.
[58]. — p. 109.

[59]. Generalitat de Catalunya, Departament de Cultura: *Arquitectura a Catalunya. L'era democrática 1977-1996*, Barcelona, 1996, p. 47.
[60]. — p. 63.

[61]. Generalitat de Catalunya: *Catalunya avui*, catalogue of the exhibition at Unesco, Paris, Generalitat de Catalunya, Barcelona, 1981, p. 55.
[62]. — *Els centres sanitaris de la Generalitat*, catalogue of the exhibition at the Colegio Oficial de Arquitectos de Barcelona, Generalitat de Catalunya, Barcelona, 1984, pp. 26-27.
[63]. — *Arquitectura sanitària i de serveis*, Generalitat de Catalunya, Barcelona, 1988, pp. 38-43.
[64]. — *Els darrers cent anys. Arquitectura i ciutat*, Generalitat de Catalunya, Barcelona, 1988, pp. 109.
[65]. — *Arquitectura d'Ensenyament*, Departament d'Ensenyament, Generalitat de Catalunya, Barcelona, 1989, pp. 57-59.
[66]. — *Quaderns de Museologia i Museografia*, n° 2, Generalitat de Catalunya, Departament de Cultura, Barcelona, 1989, pp. 40-45.
[67]. — *50 Centres d'Atenció Primària*, Departament de Sanitat i Seguretat Social, Generalitat de Catalunya, Barcelona, 1991, pp. 39.

[68]. Generalitat de Catalunya and Colegio Oficial de Arquitectos de Cataluña: *Arquitectura, obra pública en Cataluña, 1980-1985*, catalogue, Generalitat de Catalunya and COAC, Barcelona, 1985, p. 48-49.

[69]. González, Antoni; Lacuesta, Raquel: *Guia de arquitectura. Barcelona 1929-1994*, Gili, Barcelona, 1995, p. 120.
[70]. — p. 139.

[71]. Güell, Xavier; Casals, Lluis: *Casas mediterráneas en la Costa Brava*, Gili, Barcelona, 1986, p. 98-103.

[72]. Humanes, Alberto; Frechilla, Javier; Llinás, Josep: *Josep Llinás, obras y proyectos 1976-1985*, catalogue, Colegio Oficial de Arquitectos de Madrid, Madrid, 1985, p. 25.

[73]. — p. 26.
[74]. — p. 27.
[75]. — pp. 30-32.
[76]. — pp. 33-34.
[77]. — p. 35.
[78]. — pp. 36-37.
[79]. — pp. 38-41.
[80]. — pp. 42-43.
[81]. — pp. 44-48.
[82]. — pp. 49-55.
[83]. — pp. 56-65.
[84]. — pp. 66-67.
[85]. — pp. 68-93.
[86]. — pp. 94-103.
[87]. — pp. 104-112.
[88]. — pp. 113-119.

[89]. Institute Tokyo, *Urbanismo de Barcelona del último siglo*, Kajima, Tokyo, 1992.

[90]. Levene, Richard; Márquez Cecilia, Fernando; Ruiz Barbarín, Antonio: *Arquitectura española contemporánea 1975-1990*, 2 volumes, El Croquis Editorial, Madrid, 1989, pp. 63, 454-463.
[91]. — pp. 42, 608-613.

[92]. Llinás, Josep; Cavallé, Fina (Introduction): "Teatre Metropol de Tarragona. La seva restauració i reforma", *Quadern de divulgació cultural*, n° 1, Ajuntament de Tarragona, 1994.

[93]. Mancomunitat de Municipis: *Parc de Collserola*, Patronat Metropolità Parc de Collserola. Area Metropolitana de Barcelona. Barcelona, 1990, pp. 132-133.

[94]. Ministerio de Obras Públicas y Urbanismo: *Faros 89*, MOPU catalogue, Madrid, 1989, pp. 92-93.

[95]. Muntaner, Josep Maria: *Barcelona*, Taschen, Cologne, 1992, pp. 194-195.

[96]. Narbona, Cristina; Duró i Pifarrer, Jaime; Lluch, Ernest; Gil, Mª Dolores; Vázquez Molezún, Ramón; Mateo, José Luis; Botey, José María; Molinero, Jesús (Selection Committee): *I Muestra de 10 años de Arquitectura Española 1980-1990*, MOPTMA, CSCAE and UIMP, Madrid, 1991, p. 152.

[97]. Piñón, Helio: *Arquitecturas catalanas*, La Gaya Ciencia, Barcelona, 1977, pp. 166, 167, 170.
[98]. — *Nacionalisme i modernitat en l'arquitectura catalana contemporània*, Edicions 62, Barcelona, 1980, p. 139.

[99]. Quaderns (Ed.): *Guia d'arquitectura contemporània*, Quaderns, Barcelona, 1991, entry n.° A3.
[100]. — entry n.° A24.
[101]. — entry n.° B9.
[102]. — entry n.° E12.
[103]. — entry n.° F11.
[104]. — entry n.° F34.

[105]. RQP, arquitectura, s.l. and Presidencia de la Generalitat de Catalunya: *Campus, 10 anys d'arquitectura universitaria a Catalunya 1986-1996*, Barcelona, 1996, pp. 30-33.
[106]. — p. 142-145.
[107]. — p. 142, 144 and 145.

[108]. Rykwert, Joseph (Introduction); Güell, Xavier (Ed.): *Arquitectura española contemporánea. La década de los 80*, Gili, Barcelona, 1990, pp. 94-99.
[109]. — *Spanish Contemporary Architecture. The Eighties*, Gili, Barcelona, 1990, pp. 94-99.

[110]. *Wiener Architektur Seminar* (5th and 6th Viennese Seminar on Architecture), Architektur Zentrum Wien, Vienna, 1996, p. 40.
[111]. — p. 41.

Essays and Articles

Abitare, see [164].

[112]. *AMC*, Paris, 1985, n° 8, pp. 20-23.

[113]. *Architecti*, Lisbon, 1990, n° 6, pp. 70-91.
[114]. — 1990, n° 6, p. 82.
[115]. — 1990, n° 6, p. 83.
[116]. — 1990, n° 6, pp. 70-91.
[117]. — 1990, n° 6, pp. 92-98.

[118]. *Archithese,* Zurich, 1991, n° 5/91, pp. 32-33.

[119]. *Architect's Journal*, London, 1996, n° 25, p. 31.

[120]. *Architecture Magazine*, Tokyo, 1990, February 1990, p. 40.

[121]. *Arquitectos,* Consejo Superior de Colegios de Arquitectos de España, Madrid, 1994, n° 132, p. 66.
[122]. — 1994, n° 132, pp. 66-67.
[123]. — 1994, n° 132, p. 67.

[124]. *Arquitectura.* Colegio Oficial de Arquitectos de Madrid, Madrid, 1981, n° 231, pp. 33-35.
[125]. — 1987, n° 266, pp. 88-107.
[126]. — 1987, n° 269, pp. 70-79.
[127]. — 1990, n° 282, pp. 122-125.
[128]. — 1990, n° 282, pp. 126-129.

[129]. *Arquitectura Bis,* Barcelona, 1977, n° 17-18, pp. 14-15.
[130]. — 1983, n° 43, p. 27.

[131]. *Arquitectura Viva,* Madrid, 1996, n° 57-58, pp. 66-72.

[132]. *Arte y Cemento,* Bilbao, 1991, n° 1637, pp. 70-85.

Illustration Credits

[133]. *A&V,* Madrid, 1987, n° 11, pp. 74-75.
[134]. — 1990, n° 26, pp. 47-51.

[135]. *A30,* Barcelona, 1986, n° 3, p. 1-16.

[136]. *Barcelona Metropolis Mediterrània,* Ayuntamiento de Barcelona, Barcelona, 1996, n° 30, p. 4.

[137]. *Casabella,* Milan, 1987, n° 535, p. 21.
[138]. — 1996, n° 636, pp. 24-39.

[139]. *Casa Viva,* Barcelona, 1983, n° 18, pp. 18-23.

[140]. *Costruire,* Milan, 1996.

[141]. *De Architect,* The Hague, 1992, n° 47, pp. 41-43.
[142]. — 1996, n° 6, pp. 44-48.
[143]. — 1996, n° 6, p. 58.

[144]. *D'Architettura,* Avezzano, 1992, n° 7, pp. 16-21.

[145]. *Diseño Interior,* Madrid, 1993, n° 23, pp. 48-53.
[146]. — 1994, n° 35, pp. 28-35.
[147]. — 1996, n° 50, pp. 72-83.
[148]. — 1996, n° 52, pp. 56-65.
[149]. — 1996, n° 53, pp. 52-53.
[150]. — 1996, n° 54, pp. 56-65.

[151]. *Domus,* Milan, 1988, n° 696, p. 56-63.
[152]. — 1996, n° 784, pp. 36-41.

[153]. *El Croquis,* Madrid, 1985, n° 22, pp. 46-57.
[154]. — 1987, n° 29, pp. 42-51.
[155]. — 1987, n° 29, pp. 52-63.
[156]. — 1987, n° 29, pp. 64-71.
[157]. — 1988, n° 36, pp. 84-89.
[158]. — 1990, n° 43, pp. 92-103.
[159]. — 1991, n° 46, pp. 38-55.
[160]. — 1991, n° 46, pp. 56-63.
[161]. — 1995, n° 76, pp. 194-199.
[162]. — 1995, n° 76, pp. 200-205.

[163]. *Equipamientos culturales,* Madrid, 1996, n° 2, pp. 23-28.

[164]. *Abitare,* Milan, 1996 (in the press)

[165]. *Jano Arquitectura,* Barcelona, 1977, n° 44, p. 51
[166]. — 1977, n° 44, p. 45.
[167]. — 1977, n° 44, p. 48.
[168]. — 1978, n° 61, pp. 22-23.
[169]. — 1978, n° 61, pp. 24-26.
[170]. — 1978, n° 61, pp. 27-28.

[171]. *Kenchiku Bunka,* Tokyo, 1994, n° 577, pp. 55, 57.
[172]. — 1994, n° 577, pp. 52, 53, 56
[173]. — 1994, n° 577, pp. 54, 57.

[174]. *Kukan,* Tokyo, 1991, n° 6, p. 6.

[175]. — 1991, n° 6, pp. 47-49.
[176]. *L'informatiu,* Colegio de Aparejadores bimonthly publication, Barcelona, 1996, n° 93, pp. 17-23.

[177]. *Lotus International,* Milan, 1979, n° 23, p. 70.

[178]. *On Diseño,* Barcelona, 1979, special FAD issue, p. 23.
[179]. — 1988, n° 94, pp. 16-21.
[180]. — 1990, n° 116, pp. 138-147.
[181]. — 1996, n° special FAD issue, p. 54.
[182]. — 1996, n° special FAD issue, pp. 68-71.
[183]. — 1996, n° special FAD issue, pp. 76-79.
[184]. — 1996, n° 173, pp. 114-127.
[185]. — 1996, n° 173, pp. 144-149.

[186]. *Quaderns,* Barcelona, 1977, n° 125, p. 3.
[187]. — 1981, n° 144, pp. 40-42.
[188]. — 1981, n° 149, p. 61.
[189]. — 1983, n° 156, p. 14.
[190]. — 1985, n° 164, pp. 52-55.
[191]. — 1986, n° 169-170, pp. 92-95.
[192]. — 1986, n° 169-170, pp. 98-101.
[193]. — 1987, n° 172, pp. 94-98.
[194]. — 1991, n° 190, pp. 56-58.
[195]. — 1991, n° 190, pp. 59-63.
[196]. — 1993, n° 187-II, p. 44.
[197]. — 1993, n° 187-II, p. 54.
[198]. — 1993, n° 187-II, p. 59.
[199]. — 1993, n° 187-II, p. 83.
[200]. — 1993, n° 187-II, p. 88.
[201]. — 1994, n° 203, pp. 40-51.
[202]. — 1994, n° 203, pp. 52-59.
[203]. — 1994, n° 203, pp. 60-69.
[204]. — 1994, n° 203, pp. 70-74.
[205]. — 1995, n° 207-8-9, pp. 228-229.
[206]. — 1995, n° 210, pp. 78-81.
[207]. — 1996, n° 212, pp. 6-17.
[208]. — 1996, n° 212, pp. 116-145.

[209]. *Revista COA Cataluña,* Barcelona, 1989, n° 19, pp. 12-14.

[210]. *SD Review,* Tokyo, 1990, n° 9005, pp. 84-87.

[211]. *SITES,* New York, 1984, n° 12, pp. 19-22.
[212]. — 1988, n° 20, p. 67.

[213]. *The Architectural Review,* Cheshire, 1991, n° 1138, pp. 41-43.

[214]. *Techniques & Architecture,* Paris, 1996, n° 426, pp. 48-51.

[215]. *Werk, Bauen + Wohnen,* Zurich, 1991, n° 5, p. 24-27.
[216]. — 1991, n° 5, pp. 28-29.
[217]. — 1991, n° 5, p. 67.
[218]. — 1995, n° 12, pp. 32-37.

Drawings
Estudio Llinás: 64.2, 70.1, 70.2, 81.2, 81.3, 89.7, 113.5, 114.1, 122.1, 152, 153.2, 153.3, 158, 161, 162, 163, 168, 169

Photographs
Lluis Casals: 20, 22.1, 22.2, 23, 39, 41, 58/59, 62.2, 161.3, 163.1
C. Cascio/Ministerio de Fomento: 162.1
cb foto: 18/19, 28, 34, 46/47, 50.1, 50.2, 63, 157.1, 157.2, 157.3, 157.4, 158.1, 158.2, 158.3, 158.4, 159.1, 159.2, 160.1, 162.2, 162.3
COAC/Barcelona: 159.2
Ferran Freixa: 26, 27, 30/31, 32/33, 33, 35, 36.1, 36.2, 37, 53, 160.4, 161.1
Tere Isasi: 43.2, 44, 45.2, 170
Lourdes Jansana: cover, 8/9, 68, 69, 71, 72/73, 74, 75.2, 75.3, 77, 78/79, 80/81, 82.1, 82.2, 83.3, 83.4, 84, 85.2, 85.3, 86/87, 93, 98.1, 98.2, 99, 100, 101.2, 101.3, 101.4, 101.5, 102, 103, 105, 106, 107, 108.1, 108.2, 109, 115.4, 116, 117, 118/119, 120/121, 123, 124, 125, 126, 127, 128, 129, 130/131, 132, 133, 134, 135, 136.1, 136.2, 137, 138/139, 141, 142, 143, 144.1, 144.2, 145, 147.5, 147.6, 148/149, 150, 151, 164.2, 165.1, 165.2, 165.3, 165.4, 166.2, 166.3, 167.1, 167.2
Manuel Laguillo: 24/25, 29
Estudio Llinás: 89.7, 156.1, 156.2, 156.3, 156.4, 156.5, 156.6
Félix Mesalles: 15
Jordi Sarrá: 42, 43.4, 45.3, 163.3, 163.4
Hisao Suzuki: 51, 52, 55, 56, 57, 60/61, 62.1, 65, 66, 67, 88, 89.8, 90, 91, 111, 113, 114, 115.3, 160.2, 160.3, 161.2, 163.2, 164.1, 166.1

Surveys
Estudio Llinás: 18, 21.2, 21.3, 21.4, 24, 26.1, 26.2, 26.3, 27.5, 27.6, 30, 34.1, 34.2, 34.3, 34.5, 35, 38.1, 38.2, 40.1, 40.2, 40.3, 40.4, 41.6, 43.3, 46, 48.1, 48.2, 48.3, 48.4, 49.5, 49.6, 49.7, 49.8, 49.9, 49.10, 54, 56.1, 56.2, 56.3, 57.5, 57.6, 59.2, 59.3, 59.4, 59.5, 64.1, 66.1, 66.2, 66.3, 66.4, 67.5, 67.6, 67.7, 68.1, 70.3, 70.4, 70.5, 70.6, 71.7, 71.8, 71.9, 71.10, 76, 78.1, 79.2, 79.3, 86, 88.1, 88.2, 88.3, 88.4, 89.5, 92, 94.1, 94.2, 94.3, 95.4, 95.5, 95.6, 96, 97, 104, 106.2, 106.3, 106.7, 106.8, 107.4, 107.5, 107.6, 107.10, 107.11, 110.1, 110.2, 112.1, 112.2, 112.3, 113.6, 118, 122.2, 122.3, 122.4, 123.5, 123.6, 123.7, 123.9, 123.10, 130, 132.1, 132.2, 132.3, 133.4, 133.5, 133.6, 140, 142.2, 142.3, 142.4, 142.5, 143.6, 143.7, 143.8, 146.1, 146.2, 146.3, 146.4, 152, 156, 157, 158, 159, 160, 161, 162, 163, 164, 165, 166, 167, 168, 169